RICHARD GREE

THE DAZZLE and EVERETT BEEKIN

RICHARD GREENBERG is the author of *Take Me Out*, which had its U.S. premiere at the Public Theater in New York City in September 2002 after completing a critically acclaimed run at the Donmar Warehouse in London's West End and transferred to Broadway in February 2003. He is also the author of *The Dazzle* (Outer Critics Circle Award; John Gassner and Lucille Lortel nominations), *Everett Beekin*, *Three Days of Rain* (L.A. Drama Critics Award; Pulitzer Prize finalist; Olivier, Drama Desk, and Hull-Warriner nominations), *Hurrah at Last*, *Night and Her Stars*, *The American Plan*, *Life Under Water*, and *The Author's Voice*, among many other plays. His adaptation of August Strindberg's *Dance of Death* was staged on Broadway in a 2002 production starring Ian McKellen, Helen Mirren, and David Straithairn, and was produced in London's West End with Ian McKellen in Winter 2003. Mr. Greenberg received the Oppenheimer Award for best new playwright as well as the first PEN/Laura Pels Award for a playwright in midcareer. He is an associate artist at the South Coast Repertory and a member of the Ensemble Studio Theatre. He lives in New York City.

THE
DAZZLE

AND

EVERETT

BEEKIN

FABER AND FABER, INC.

AN AFFILIATE OF FARRAR, STRAUS AND GIROUX

NEW YORK

THE DAZZLE

❀ AND ❀

EVERETT BEEKIN

TWO PLAYS BY

RICHARD GREENBERG

FABER AND FABER, INC.
An affiliate of Farrar, Straus and Giroux
19 Union Square West, New York 10003

Distributed in Canada by Penguin Books of Canada Limited
Printed in the United States of America
FIRST EDITION, 2003

Library of Congress Cataloging-in-Publication Data
Greenberg, Richard, 1958–
    The dazzle; and, Everett Beekin : two plays / by Richard Greenberg.— 1st ed.
    p. cm.
    ISBN 0-571-21123-2
    I. Title: The dazzle; and, Everett Beekin.   II. Greenberg, Richard, 1958–
Everett Beekin.   III. Title: Everett Beekin.   IV. Title.

PS3557.R3789 E95 2003
813'.54—dc21

                                                    2002192538

Designed by Gretchen Achilles

www.fsgbooks.com

10   9   8   7   6   5   4   3   2   1

THE DAZZLE
is for Peter Frechette, Reg Rogers,
Francie Swift, and David Warren

EVERETT BEEKIN
is for Shirley Levine Greenberg

CONTENTS

THE
DAZZLE

AUTHOR'S NOTE

THE DAZZLE is based on the lives of the Collyer brothers, about whom I know almost nothing.

THE DAZZLE was produced in March 2002 in New York City by the Roundabout Theatre Company, Todd Haimes, artistic director; Ellen Richard, managing director; Julia C. Levy, executive director, external affairs. It was directed by David Warren; set design was by Allen Moyer; lighting design was by Jeff Croiter; costume design was by Gregory A. Gale; and sound design was by Robert Murphy. Original music was by Lawrence Yurman; musical staging was by Karen Azenberg. The production stage manager was Jay Adler. The casting was by Amy Christopher and Bernard Telsey Casting.

The cast was as follows:

LANGLEY COLLYER
Reg Rogers

HOMER COLLYER
Peter Frechette

MILLY ASHMORE
Francie Swift

The play was originally presented by the New York Stage and Film Company and the Powerhouse Theatre at Vassar in July 2000.

SETTING

The Collyer mansion in New York City. Early to mid
twentieth century. Bric-a-brac. Later, impassable mountains
of bric-a-brac.

CHARACTERS

LANGLEY COLLYER

HOMER COLLYER

MILLY ASHMORE

❋ ACT ONE ❋

SCENE 1

LANG *bursts in, followed by* HOMER *and* MILLY, *all in formal dress.*

LANG I didn't hold the last note long enough!

HOMER You're mad—

LANG Not long—not *half* long enough—

MILLY We didn't hear it that way—

LANG My foot slipped from the pedal—dead air, all of a sudden, everywhere—

MILLY However, I'm sure you're right—

LANG *(at one of the pianos)* I went *(plays, sings)* DA DA *DA.*

HOMER As it was notated in the score; precisely—

MILLY That doesn't matter—

LANG And it should have been at *least*: DA DA DAAAAAAAAAAAAA . . . *(trails the note forever)*

HOMER *(after the last vibration dies)* Well, there, you've made it right.

LANG There is no making it right—

MILLY No, how could there be?

LANG It's not the same thing—it's not the same phrase. Don't you hear? This *(plays phrase)* is not the same as *this*. *(plays identical phrase identically)* Don't you hear? This *(again)* is not the same as this. *(again)* *(Beat.)* This *(again)* is not the same as this. *(again)* *(Beat.)*

This *(again)* is not the same as this. *(again)*

(Pause.)

MILLY *(thrilled)* I understand you!

HOMER Well, you're a great bore who's had an enormous success.

LANG This *(again)* is not the same—

HOMER Oh, shut up.

MILLY It was an enormous success, but your dissatisfaction is even more thrilling!

LANG I didn't hold the note long enough—

HOMER Langley, on the platform, you held the note as long as any of us could stand it; just now you've held the same note even longer, and it's brought us all to the point of complete nervous collapse. Now, please, let us *move on* . . .

LANG It wasn't the same passage, Homer—

HOMER It was exactly the same passage—

LANG No, not the same, just *identical* . . .

HOMER Ah.

MILLY Oh.

Marvelous!

I love what you've done with this place.

HOMER Ha-HA!

MILLY Why do you laugh?

HOMER Oh, I wasn't, I was hawking.

MILLY Why are there two pianos, though?

LANG The other is out of tune.

MILLY Can't you have it tuned?

LANG Of *course* not.

HOMER *(sitting down to read)* Can I get you a book, Lang? Something so you can read yourself to sleep?

MILLY You have a guest here, Mr.— Homer, that is.

HOMER Oh yes. So sorry *(mock cordial)*, Miss Ashmore.

MILLY Not at all.

HOMER Can I get you something? Comic book? The Koran?

MILLY Does one come back to your home only to be offered books and magazines? Isn't conversation expected; perhaps a cordial or a cigarette?

HOMER Hard to say, the situation is unprecedented. *(LANG starts to laugh.)* Oh, look, ol' gloomy Gus has cracked a smile *(LANG goes poker-faced.)* and off it comes. My brother is *méchant*. Do you know the word *"méchant"*?

MILLY I've been to France.

HOMER Oh yes? Oh really? Oh well, I've been to America, yet I don't know the word *(His finger runs down a column in the open pedestal dictionary.)* "meristem." "The unformed growing cellular tissue of the younger part of plants"—well, now I *do* know it. However, I suppose France is an older country with a more rudimentary vocabulary. At any *rate*: my brother is *méchant*. He is *insupportable*; he is *incorrigible*—

MILLY Your brother is an artist.

LANG *(quietly)* Don't say that.

MILLY And so if he needs to maintain two pianos, one permanently untuned, it should be accepted, unquestioned. We have two pianos also, but they're on quite separate floors.

LANG Is one a spinet?

MILLY Yes . . .

LANG And do you—the family—your family, that is—the
members of your family, that is—by which I mean the males
and the females, that is—do you *group* around the spinet—
around the piano *and* the bench, that is—and does one of
you play—or do you alternate—or do some combination of
you alternate—playing—and the rest of you—or *all* of you,
including the one who plays—*sing*?

MILLY . . . Yes.

LANG Or do one—or some of—you—have a wretched voice or
wretched voices—and attempt—or attempts—to sing but
fail, or stay silent utterly, or do—all of that—in some—
combination?

MILLY I—

HOMER Are they songs about poor maidens selling baked
potatoes from the curb?

LANG Homer—please—you're going too *fast*—

HOMER I merely—

LANG She hasn't—had a chance—to answer me yet—

HOMER All right, Lang—

LANG I haven't been answered yet—

HOMER All *right*, Lang—

LANG Answer me.

(Beat.)

MILLY *(brightly)* Would you mind, terribly, repeating the
question?

LANG *(sadly)* I can't.

MILLY Oh, don't look that way, it makes you ugly, and you were
so beautiful tonight—

LANG No—

MILLY Yes—you looked dashing . . .

LANG Dashing?

MILLY Yes!

LANG Did you hear that, Home? I'm dashing!

HOMER PUH!

MILLY Am I really not to get a cordial of some kind?

HOMER Of course.

  I bid you a cordial adieu.

MILLY A drink. I'd like a drink.

HOMER Is it that you find rudeness stylish in some way?

MILLY Yes.

HOMER And you want to be stylish?

MILLY Yes.

HOMER So the more I try to get rid of you, the likelier you are
  to stay?

MILLY There must be a bottle of something somewhere. I'm not
  fussy.

HOMER Hm. *(Beat; mock-fancy.)* I believe there's some
  absinthe in the mudroom.

He rises, goes.

MILLY He likes me so much.

LANG Oh.

MILLY What are you looking at?

LANG A thread.

MILLY Where?

LANG In the antimacassar.

MILLY Which thread?

LANG That one.

MILLY The blue one?

LANG *(sighs)* Yes. I suppose that's all we have time to call it.

MILLY Tell me: What does your brother do?

LANG . . . I don't . . . How do you mean . . . what do you
    mean?—
MILLY His occupation.
LANG Oh! Oh . . . He's an admiralty lawyer—
MILLY Really? My, that sounds exciting!
LANG Yes—the books often have—lovely bindings—retired,
    now.
MILLY Retired? So young a man? Why?
        (LANG *sighs.*)
        That is a characteristic noise of yours, isn't it?
LANG What?
MILLY *(imitates his sigh)*
LANG Yes.
MILLY Why?
LANG People ask me questions—
MILLY People ask everybody questions.
LANG I don't have wind enough for a single complete answer.
        That would seem to be the difference.
MILLY Do you like me?
LANG . . . Yes.
MILLY That's all the answer I need.
LANG That was a yes-or-no question.
MILLY I'm going to ask you a harder one. What do you like
    about me?
LANG *(sighs)*
MILLY More than that. Tell me. I'm not expecting a complete
    answer. I'd find a complete answer insulting. Tell me a little:
    What do you like about me?
LANG I find your money thrilling, and I'm fond of your hair.
MILLY *(on to him)* Which hair?

LANG *(points)* That one.

But even that's a group.

MILLY *(leans over and kisses him)* Did you mind my doing that?

LANG It was all right.

MILLY Touch my hair.

LANG *(baffled for choice)* Uuuhh . . .

MILLY Start with your favorite . . .

(He puts his hand to a ringlet, caresses it.)

That's nice.

It's so strange you like my money.

I've always rather detested it, myself.

LANG *(neutrally)* That's stupid.

MILLY Well, I have. It's not mine, yet one day it will be mine, although I've never done anything to earn it—

LANG It's in something like—tallow—or gypsum—isn't it?

MILLY Something like.

LANG Yes—something where there are *fields*—or *mines* or caverns—and laborers go—*out*—to them—

MILLY Ha-ha—

LANG —and labor in them—and then come back with their *plunder*—

MILLY Yes, I come from robbers, long lines of robbers, unconscionable—

LANG —and never—do they—think of the fields whence the plunder comes—do they?—

MILLY They're horribly exploited—

LANG But—am I right? Do they—really—just come home—or go to—pubs—and drink beer and eat oysters and *forget*? Is that it?

MILLY Well, I can hardly be expected to know what goes on in the minds of some grubby workers—but—probably—yes—I mean, they're dumb as posts, for the most part.

LANG That must be nice.

I would like to be one of them.

MILLY Idiotic idea!

LANG Why?

MILLY You could no more be a laborer than I could—

LANG I didn't say I *could* be, I said I would *like* to be—

MILLY That sort of thing should revolt you; it's the very opposite of you—

LANG Those two ideas don't go together—why wouldn't I want to be the opposite of myself? I don't propose my character as an ideology—it's a condition—it's my condition—it wasn't chosen, it wasn't elected by— Although you're right, I don't like to sweat.

(Pause. He continues to fondle her curl, staring at it.)

At seven P.M. most nights . . .

At seven P.M. most *week*nights . . .

I sit in that window—*that* window—

At seven P.M. most weeknights, I will sit in the wing chair in that window and stare through the window, the evening paper propped in my lap, as a sop to the neighbors—who might be—sometimes *are*—have, at any rate, *begun* to— stare back—and I'll watch the men return from business.

Especially this is in late fall, and early winter—coats are important—thick collars turned up—and a current of wind—a light current of wind that seems—this is an illusion—that seems to speed them along.

They are accompanied by leaves. Curled umber and

orange and sepia at their feet, sped by the wind—that's *not* an illusion. Lit torchères in the neighbor's windows—dogs— I'm sorry, I meant to warn you, this is a *sentimental* story. And the men—what I mean is, their lower extremities all, what I'm trying to say is: their *gait* is terribly relaxed. As they approach their own houses, the day of business behind them, whiskey waiting—I've seen that through the window, that's *not* illusion—roasts of beef—and oh—well— children— And as they walk—stride—almost skip—their marvelous chins goosing butterflies—their wooden sticks and leather bags jaunting forth—it's a kind of unleafing of the day—it borders on the visible, how they scatter behind them what's come before—at seven P.M. as they approach their homes—via the River Lethe—ha-ha!—and they will sometimes catch my eye—and nod to me!—as if we were the neighbors that we are—as if what is *were*—as if this were *my* seven P.M., too—a little nod—and I'm swung into the circle of their hour—but then that stops—and the next hour is smashed to smithereens—like my aunt Prudy's cheap lacquered vase— *(Beat.)*

MILLY I come from swine.

No, I live among the most remarkably unpleasant people.

What time is it? I stay out so late all the time so as not to have to return to Fifth Avenue.

You don't know what a hell it is there!

Oh, it's so lovely, your poetry of seven P.M.! But I've spent that same hour cowering in an upstairs room, cowering with the lamp unlit, hiding . . . hoping for . . . something . . .
(She takes his hand and puts it on her breast.)

LANG No, I'm not done here yet.

(He puts his hand back on her hair.)

MILLY You're a miracle, Lang. *My* miracle. I've lived most of my
life in a kind of sleepy terror. With you, I'm afraid but
completely awake! I never know what you'll do or what you
mean. You disconnect everything.

LANG Yes. It's like how menacing a man can seem, pausing on
the sidewalk at a peculiar angle, until you realize he's
walking a very low dog.

HOMER *enters, carrying a bottle and glasses.*

HOMER I couldn't find anything.

MILLY Anything?

HOMER To drink.

He places the glasses on the table and pours one drink.

MILLY Nothing of any kind?

HOMER No.

MILLY No beverage of any kind?

HOMER So terribly sorry. None.

(He swallows and lets out a satisfied breath.)

MILLY Well, that's all right. I'm not really thirsty.

HOMER Langley.

LANG Yes, Homer.

HOMER Remove your hand from that lady's coiffure.

LANG But I almost have a name for its color.

HOMER No one cares.

LANG *I* do.

HOMER That is not sufficient reason to keep it up. Please.

　　(LANG *takes his hand out of her hair. The hand*
　　trembles.)

　　　　Thank you.

(Pause.)

MILLY *(pours herself a drink)* How exciting it must have
　　been. Admiralty law, I mean.

HOMER Why?

MILLY I think the sea is the most exciting thing! The air, all
　　salt, all brackish, and then the weather vanes and . . .
　　nor'easters and whatnot— Isn't it? Didn't you find?

HOMER Admiralty lawyers do not sail.

(Beat.)

LANG You did—

HOMER What?

LANG —*stand* on a battleship, once, and have your
　　photograph taken . . . Didn't you?

(A smile blooms slowly between them.)

MILLY Why did you give it up?

(HOMER looks at her. He takes the glass from her hand.)

HOMER I was needed here.

MILLY For what reason?

HOMER *(crossing to LANG)* I am my brother's *(hands him the*
　　glass) . . . accountant.

SCENE.

SCENE 2

HOMER *storming;* LANG *playing a lugubriously slow and unrecognizable piece on the piano.*

HOMER You *must* listen! You must take this in, Lang! You cannot keep up this *policy* of *caprice* with your booking agents! Your position is not so secure as all that, you know; your reputation is a little teetery—they will drop you, do you understand? Drop you cold if you keep withdrawing like this—at a moment's notice and on the flimsiest of pretexts. "I have a cold in the nose." You don't *play* with your nose— although at this rate, that will come next! At least—say— something—like—oh! "An andiron fell across my wrist," or somesuch, and we can make a splint and *show* them something—but it seems to them like actual spite. As if you're playing out some sort of contempt. You cannot do that, Lang. These are agents, managers, functionaries in the world of art, they already suspect themselves of being louts, if you confirm it for them, they'll make you *pay*—which brings me to my *next* point—which is, we have *bills* to pay, and if you think we're bottomlessly rich, let me disabuse you right— Do you think when our parents moved to Harlem it represented a *burgeoning* of the family fortune, because— and—oh, yes—this house is *big*—but that's because the neighborhood might as well be Praetoria—as convenient as it is to where—things are really *happening*— You—once you seemed to have some *sense* of—what was what—but with every passing day, you become—more and more—less and *less*—sensible, I mean—and meanwhile, *I'm* left with the paperwork, with the mounting debt, with the task of diplomacy—even in the neighborhood—the butter-and-egg men do not hold us *dear*, really, they could do very nicely without our custom—especially when we're in arrears to them—well, the way you *sniff* the eggs—what are they supposed to think? Really, Lang, you have no idea what I go through in the course of a—day—your circumference, I know, is *vast*, but my circuit is intricate—and debilitating—and I'm only asking for you to cooperate—a little bit—with— IS THIS "THE MINUTE WALTZ"?

LANG Yes.

(He plays the last note. It lingers forever.)

HOMER Oh God, we're doomed.

LANG Were you speaking to me before?

HOMER Yes.

LANG I wasn't listening.

(Beat.)

HOMER Ah.

LANG I was playing.

HOMER Yes. I heard. It was very impressive. You completed "The Minute Waltz" in slightly under three quarters of an hour—

LANG It was quite nice—

HOMER Next year this time, you'll have to take an intermission.

LANG Are you *upset*?

HOMER . . . Of course not.

LANG You are, though. I think you are. Why? Be specific.

HOMER No reason. No reason at all.

LANG It doesn't have anything to do with me, does it?

HOMER How could it?

> *(Pause.)*
>
> You need to get things under control, Lang.

LANG What things?

HOMER You need— Are you listening to me now?

LANG Yes—

HOMER Are you really?

LANG I'm not playing—

HOMER All right. You need to—not even in your *head*—

LANG I promise you, Homer, you are my only music at the moment.

HOMER You need to—conduct yourself in a more— Well, *don't* listen like *that*—please—

LANG Like what?

HOMER With such—rapt—concentration—

LANG Why not?

HOMER Because in the first place, I'm not going to say anything delightful. In the second place, there are—there *should* be—natural modulations to—the art of listening— and, in the third place—it's just creepy.

LANG I'm sorry, Homer.

HOMER That's—fine—look—you have to conduct your business in a more businesslike way.

LANG Ah. *(Beat.)* I don't know what that means.

HOMER It means—for example—you have to stick to your word.

LANG I do stick to my word, Homer—

HOMER Lang—

LANG Or—well—actually—it's more like my *words* stick to *me*—I mean—I speak in a kind of stream—and usually—I try to do whatever it was I said last.

HOMER That's not how business is conducted.

LANG It *ought* to be.

HOMER But it *can't*. If in September of 1904 you promise to perform Schubert at such-and-such a place in August of 1905, you are expected to perform Schubert at such-and-such a place in August of 1905.

LANG Well, that's ridiculous.

HOMER It isn't.

LANG It *is*, and I'm not going to explain why, because I just don't have the wind for it at the moment. You should know anyway, Homer; you should know why.

(Beat. HOMER *sits.)*

HOMER Do you want to be old and sick and hungry and without a home?

LANG I can't say, I haven't tried.

HOMER *Would you please care enough about me to accept a premise?*

LANG . . . Yes, Homer, I'm sorry.

HOMER We are not in trouble at the moment—

LANG Then may I go?

HOMER But we *may be* shortly.

LANG . . . Hm.

Ah. How shortly?

HOMER I don't— Does it matter?

LANG Yes.

HOMER *Very* shortly.

LANG "Very." Timid, empty, stark little word.

HOMER Tomorrow, the day after, ten years from now—all I am saying is we have to take *the long view*—

LANG *(returns to piano, plays a chord, holds it)*

HOMER *Lang!*

LANG Do you hear that—

HOMER All Harlem hears that—

LANG . . . If that were true . . .

HOMER I am so sick of these chords you bang out—at random—night and day—they reverberate endlessly— they've worked their way into the curtains, I swear it, like some old bad stench of cigar smoke, or—

LANG Most smells are actually pleasant if you don't know where they're coming from.

HOMER *(slams hands onto piano top)* Lang!

LANG . . . Yes, Homer?

HOMER What do you think of the girl?

LANG What girl?

HOMER Oh Lord—the girl—the girl—the rich girl—who sits beside me at your recitals—and swoons and gasps and sways as though she were the music—what do you think of her?

LANG Mildred.

HOMER Yes.

LANG Milly.

HOMER Yes.

LANG Her name is Milly.

HOMER That does not constitute an opinion.

LANG Doesn't it?

HOMER I believe that she's in love with you.

(Pause.)

LANG Huh.

Is that . . . ?

Really.

HOMER I believe so.

LANG What does that mean?

Tell me exactly.

Turn on the lamps first.

HOMER It isn't dark.

LANG It will be when you finish.

HOMER I am not going to go . . . into all that.

LANG Why not?

HOMER Because . . . it isn't definable.

LANG Then on what authority do you speak of it?

HOMER One can . . . *feel* it without . . . being able to . . . put
into words—

LANG I don't agree—I think a word can exist without a
meaning, but a meaning can't exist without a word—music
is better than either, because it forgoes both—that's why I
hate books—books always seem to me like music explaining
itself under duress. But what were you saying?

HOMER I don't remember.

LANG Love! That was it. You were going to define it.

HOMER I was attempting *not* to—

LANG Because you've never experienced it?

(Beat.)

HOMER You live only to torture me, don't you?

LANG Not at all.

HOMER I *have*—experienced—

LANG Oh pooh— *Where? When?*

HOMER Lang—

LANG When you were away?

HOMER Yes.

LANG When you were away in— Oh, what is China always called in the disintegrating books—*Cathay*?

HOMER Among other places.

LANG Really?

HOMER Yes.

LANG Really?

HOMER Yes!

LANG Oh, Homer, why must you lie *at home*? Lying is for outdoors—this is our house!

HOMER I am *not*— I have a very real past—

LANG There is no such thing—

HOMER I . . . have . . . had . . . have had . . . one.

For all the good it does me now.

I was . . . a different person. Before.

You must grant me that, it's my solace.

Oh Christ Christ Christ Christ, why are we— *(Pause. He sits.)* I know you can't answer this next question, but I'll ask it anyway: Do you love her?

LANG Oh, I can answer that.

HOMER You can?

LANG Yes. I know what love is; you're the one who can't define it.

Do I love her?

Yes.

I believe I do.

HOMER Truly?

LANG Yes.

I believe so.

There's something . . . miasmic about her.

HOMER Miasmic?

LANG Yes. It's her speech! It's when she speaks. You see, she
has nothing to say; and she says it incessantly. There's never
a phrase, a word—an accent, even—that hasn't been
thoroughly modified by convention, made virtually inaudible
by overuse. She's so ordinary! It's as though ordinariness has
been rubbed into the very *nap* of her voice—her voice lulls
me! It has none of the hooks and snares of most voices—
Why, Homer, she very nearly bores me, and hardly anything
does that! I can imagine living with her as one would beside
a narrow and uninteresting body of water—scarcely even
aware of its existence—yet made utterly tranquil by its flow.
  Yes. I love her.
  And sex is not a problem for me, you know. I mean, it's no
more intense than anything else.
(Pause.)
HOMER Well, then . . .
LANG Why do you ask?
HOMER No reason.
  (Beat.)
  She's very rich.
  (Beat.)
  No reason.

SCENE.

SCENE 3

Offstage, a string quartet plays a waltz. People dance. Light slips in under the doors. The doors burst open: MILLY *and* LANG *enter, laughing, in formal party dress.*

MILLY Oh, what a funny idea!

LANG What?

MILLY This! This party here! It's—

LANG The music is—

MILLY —in the Collyer manse—of all places—

LANG —excruciating—

MILLY It's—no—very sweet—a string quartet—

LANG The cello is flat—

MILLY No one minds—

LANG —a sixty-fourth tone flat—

MILLY A sixty-*fourth* tone!

LANG Yes.

MILLY There is no such thing as a sixty-fourth tone—

LANG There is.

MILLY People can't *hear* a sixty-fourth tone.

LANG Other people.

MILLY Don't listen.

LANG I can't help it—

MILLY *(kisses him)* Don't. Why are you having this party?

LANG It was my brother's—

MILLY At my family's, by the way, there's an orchestra—

LANG It was Homer's idea—

MILLY A full symphony orchestra—

LANG He thinks we need to woo the neighbors—Christmas! He thinks like that. He has a holiday mentality. He thinks in great chunks of time, punctuated by the advent of God.

MILLY Well, people do.

LANG He's terribly excited lately—he thinks we're becoming banal—the prospect exhilarates him—

MILLY I'm so glad to be here, with you, and not at home with all the horrible, horrible people. Thank you for inviting me.

LANG It was Homer's idea.

MILLY Really.

LANG It's part of his new life. He's having a new life. It's all very funny, but we mustn't giggle about it in his presence.

    Do you like the neighbors?

MILLY They seem—

LANG They don't care for me.

MILLY I'm sure—

LANG And this is an ever—worsening—situation— I think we're in bad credit or something—with some of them—and that makes the others—gabble—about us—although Homer, I think, I think Homer is all right—still—beside the pale, not yet beyond it—isn't it funny?—when they all seem to me— harrowingly peculiar—but I'm—apparently not—to judge—

HOMER *enters.*

HOMER *(to* MILLY*)* You're not drinking.

    You must let me get you something—

MILLY We're fine—

HOMER We?

Are we speaking the language of "we"?

MILLY For the evening.

HOMER Life has become a three-volume novel.

MILLY Hardly.

HOMER That's all right—it's what I'd hoped—*it's what I'd hoped!*

He exits.

MILLY Your brother—

LANG He is—

MILLY Last year I visited Vienna—they're doing marvelous things in the mental field—it might behoove him to—

LANG Oh, please, no.

MILLY Lang, you might have noticed I have some very modern ideas—

LANG No. I never noticed you had *any* ideas.

MILLY . . . Nevertheless.

LANG That doesn't mean—

MILLY Nevertheless, I—

LANG That doesn't mean that you *lack* them—

MILLY —No—I—

LANG Only that I don't care about any ones you may have.

MILLY *My point is* . . . I might be a bit much for you to take in all at once.

LANG Everything is a bit much for me to take in all at once.

MILLY I mean . . . *I* might be . . . in particular.

LANG Everything is particular. You're a little less so. That's why I can be with you.

MILLY . . . I don't know how to make out . . . what you're saying
to me—

LANG That can be a problem.

MILLY You seem to speak entirely in . . . strategies . . .

LANG No, you're wrong. I speak in rocks.

MILLY Rocks?

LANG Yes. Rocks: my words are not absolutely solid, but near
as it gets.

MILLY But I think sometimes what you say—insults me—

LANG No, you're wrong. To insult someone is to aim for his
feelings—I never aim for people's feelings—I never do
anything with people's feelings, I leave them alone, like
books.

MILLY Interesting. *(re: the music)* Oh, this one—I love this
waltz—

LANG Yes—it's even nicer in tune—

MILLY Can we dance?

LANG I doubt it.

MILLY *(opening her arms)* Lang.

LANG No. I doubt it.

MILLY Please try.

LANG *sighs and enters her arms. She leads. She dances in
tempo to the music; he goes only half that rate.*

You're dragging the tempo.

LANG No, I'm perfectly in tempo—it's you and the musicians
who're going wrong. *(She tries to speed him and he pulls
away, continues dancing alone, at his rate.)* It's better
this way.

MILLY All right.

(He dances alone. She dances alone, twice as fast.)

This is nice.

LANG Much nicer.

MILLY But I miss holding you.

LANG Hmmm . . .

MILLY And you miss me.

LANG I do?

MILLY Yes.

LANG Oh.

MILLY The feel of me.

LANG I miss that?

MILLY Yes.

LANG Oh.

MILLY You miss it severely.

LANG Really?

MILLY Yes.

LANG I didn't know.

MILLY Well, now you do.

LANG Thank you. I'm grateful for the information.

MILLY Lang?

LANG Yes.

MILLY You dance divinely.

LANG Yes. That would be the only explanation.

MILLY Lang?

LANG Yes?

MILLY Your brother, Homer?

LANG That's not a question; why did your voice go up?

MILLY Why do you suppose he is to me as he is to me?

LANG I don't know what you just said.

MILLY His behavior toward me is positively schizophrenic.

LANG Lord, that's an interesting word!

(HOMER appears on the mezzanine, unseen by them.)

MILLY He shuns me, then he courts me—do you suppose there's something in his past—some deep aftertrace from his childhood that he sees replicated in me and that he's trying to banish or fix in some way?

LANG . . . Hmm?

MILLY I said—

LANG Homer is having a tragedy. He's a tragic figure. We are, apparently. If I start to giggle, please excuse me. *(He dances half the tempo again, virtually at a stop. She speeds slightly.)*

MILLY In what way tragic?

LANG Oh, I don't know. I don't understand these things. What is tragedy? I wrote it in a notebook once.

MILLY Tragedy is—a feeling more than any—

LANG Oh, yes, I remember! Tragedy is when a *few* people sink to the level where *most* people always *are.* That's what's happened to him—to us! That's why he's, what, sycophantic—

MILLY Schizophrenic—

LANG Polysyllabic. This is all nonsense, though. You make me speak nonsense. It's pleasant.

MILLY What is the nature of the tragedy?

LANG Oh—I don't—don't ask that so passionately—as if it were—as if it *were*— Financial, I—

MILLY Financial reversals?

LANG Homer promises we'll end starving in the gutter. I find that provocative.

MILLY And now he's suddenly kind to me.

LANG Is he? Well, good. *(She has paused.)* Why have you stopped dancing? The excruciating music plays on—

MILLY Lang?

LANG Another rhetorical question.

Yes. I am.

MILLY This dress I'm wearing?

LANG *(in imitation)* These shoes I've donned?

MILLY It's very cunningly made.

LANG Yes.

MILLY It wraps and wraps.

LANG I like—the way that happens—

MILLY —and unwraps—and unwraps—

LANG Which will make it possible for you to bathe!

MILLY *(unwrapping from the top)* There's a wonderful feel to it—would you like to feel?

LANG I don't know that—I have the time—

MILLY It's silk—silk against my skin—did we lock those doors?

LANG No.

MILLY No matter. Won't these layers look marvelous on the floor?

LANG Against the Oriental rug, yes. *(He tries to dance again, stops.)*

Yes.

MILLY Yes. Textures are endlessly fascinating, don't you think?

LANG I . . .

MILLY Combined. Revealed. *(She is now topless.)* Don't you think?

LANG God.

MILLY Lang.

LANG You are—

MILLY Lang—

LANG Such a *fact*—standing there—

MILLY Do you want to touch? Would you like to touch?

LANG . . . Yes.

MILLY You may.

LANG May I.

MILLY Yes.

He goes to her, drops to his knees, buries his head in her dress.

HOMER Not the *dress*, idiot, the *girl*!

LANG Homer!

HOMER You've misunderstood.

LANG You should—cover up—

MILLY That's all right—

HOMER *(descending)* Not on my account—

MILLY That's all right—I don't mind—

HOMER No need to cover up on my account—

LANG We didn't—know you were there—

MILLY I did—

LANG —You?—

MILLY I saw.

HOMER And you—stripped—anyway?

MILLY I thought it was what you wanted—

HOMER What I—?

MILLY —wanted—

HOMER What does that have to do with anything?

MILLY I thought it was what Lang wanted—

HOMER What Lang wanted?

MILLY It was for the greater good of you both. And it was what
    I wanted.

(Beat.)

HOMER *Fix* yourself.

(Pause.)

MILLY Yes. All right. *(She pulls up the dress; it covers her loosely.)* There. Is that worse?

LANG Much worse.

MILLY Hmm.

LANG Much, much worse. All disappeared.

MILLY Sit beside me.

LANG Taken back.

MILLY Sit beside me, you can hold my dress.

(He sits beside her.)

HOMER *(lights a cigar)* We are having a grand success tonight, Lang. We are gone from the bottom to the top in the neighbors' estimation. Before they reviled us as scum, and now they resent us as gentry. Could there be a more satisfactory—

MILLY May I have a cigar?

HOMER No.
   Yes, a grand success. Very exciting. We'll be welcomed with open arms. By all these dreadful people. These cretins, these merchants, these sultans of dry goods and dairy.
   We've triumphed in Lilliput! Who'd have thought it possible even a week ago?

MILLY Your fortunes have reversed in reverse.

HOMER Exactly! Our fortunes have reversed in reverse.
   (Another piece starts playing.)
   Oh, this one is lovely.
   Oh, I remember this one.

(MILLY starts to dress more completely.)

LANG Do you remember it from— Where do you remember it?

HOMER Long ago.

LANG Cathay!

HOMER *(starts dancing)* Yes, Cathay!

MILLY Oh, have you been to China! I went as a girl, a young girl—

HOMER *(dances twice as fast as the music)* Yes!

MILLY It was so lovely, I thought—so brutal—

HOMER Yes—I was there—dance with me!

MILLY Really?

HOMER Yes—dance with me! Please—I love the whole thing of parlors—and music drifting from nearby rooms—and lighting!

MILLY All right. *(She tries to enter his arms; he's going too fast.)*

HOMER And when I was in China, I met a girl—

LANG Oh, dear—

MILLY Could you slow down—

HOMER A lovely young girl—

MILLY What was her name?

HOMER Her name?

MILLY Yes—what— I'm going to have to *lunge* at—

LANG Cio-Cio-San—

MILLY *(throws herself into his arms)* Cio-Cio-San?

HOMER Yes.

MILLY That sounds familiar.

HOMER We *were* familiar.

MILLY Are you sure that's a *Chi*nese name?

LANG Cathay! Cathay!

MILLY Are you dancing a polka? Because they're playing a waltz.

HOMER And she loved me absolutely.

MILLY That's nice.

HOMER Horribly, terribly, and we would "dance"—

MILLY That's—

HOMER But I seduced and abandoned her—

MILLY Oh, dear.

HOMER I was handsome then. And Caucasian. And I could do
that sort of thing. It was acceptable.

MILLY Why are you dancing so fast?

HOMER She had my child—I left her—sometimes I wonder
what became of her—I'll have to go back someday—and
see—

MILLY Wait a second.

(They stop dancing.)

HOMER . . . What?

MILLY That story—

HOMER . . . Yes?

MILLY It's from a play! I saw that story in a play! Last season.

HOMER You might have seen something like it on the stage—

MILLY It! It! It! The very thing—the whole thing—only she was
*Nippo*nese—not *Chi*nese—

HOMER There might have been something along those lines on
the Broadway stage—such things have been known to—

MILLY The Thing Itself! The Thing Itself!

HOMER It's—possible—

MILLY It was in a play. It was something contrived by a
playwright—

HOMER Well, where do you think he got the idea?

MILLY I— Well—he contrived it—

HOMER Out of what?

MILLY His— Well—his imagination!

HOMER His *imagination*! We're talking about a *play*wright!
Playwrights don't have imaginations—they're drunken

illiterates, every last one of— Look: here's what happened—
I *met* this man one day—

MILLY Where?

HOMER Where?

MILLY Yes, where?

HOMER At . . . *(to* LANG*)* Help me.

LANG An oyster bar.

HOMER Yes! At an oyster bar. And I was feeling a bit maudlin.
And I began to tell him my story—

MILLY So then that play was drawn from life?

HOMER From my life, yes—

MILLY I saw it; it didn't *seem* drawn from life—

HOMER That's no concern of mine; that's failure of craft—

MILLY Although the scenery did— Lord, that was realistic! Do
you know they employed actual termites to get an
authentically termite-eaten look? Except they had to keep
rebuilding because the walls kept falling on the actors'
heads—

HOMER Well, it was my story.

MILLY I don't believe it.

HOMER Then you're an imbecile—

MILLY I don't be—

HOMER I was paid for it!

MILLY Paid for it?

HOMER Five dollars. Right then. He said, "Young man, let me
have that story—I'm a drunken and illiterate playwright,
and *that* story is the freshest thing I've—"

MILLY What a lot of—

HOMER And he gave me five dollars on the spot.

LANG On the spot?

HOMER On the spot!

MILLY I bet.

HOMER You still don't believe me?

MILLY No.

HOMER *(takes out billfold)* Well . . . *(throws a five-dollar bill on the table) What* do you *say* to *that?*

LANG Lord! Then it must all be true!

HOMER I think I'm due an apology—

MILLY I think—.

HOMER I think I'm due a *formal* apology—

MILLY I think not— I think—

HOMER Well, then, stop smoking my cigar!

MILLY You wouldn't give me one—

HOMER In that case—stop—oh! There must be *something* I can take away from you!

MILLY There isn't.

HOMER There must be.

MILLY That's—

HOMER There *must* be—

MILLY No. That's the fact about me.

(Beat. LANG *storms up, lunges at the piano.)*

LANG THIS IS BARBARIC!

MILLY What is?

LANG This chaos they're calling music!

He plays the same piece the quartet is playing but at half tempo.

HOMER Oh, that's much better. *(He rises and once again dances at double the quartet tempo.)*

MILLY I love dance parties! *(She rises and dances to the quartet.)*

HOMER Yes! I remember them from long ago! I MUST SEE TO OUR GUESTS!

He swirls off through the double doors.
MILLY *stops dancing.* LANG *looks up, stops playing, sits there. Pause.*

MILLY Tell me exactly what you're thinking.

LANG All girls ask that question.

MILLY We do.

LANG It's a preposterous question.

MILLY Answer it anyway.

LANG I'm thinking: I wish I didn't have so many senses.

MILLY So many—?

LANG Five. Five is far too many. I wish I could lose one.

MILLY What else?

LANG Oh.

　　(Beat.)

That I had a minute in college when . . . it seemed . . .

MILLY Seemed—?

LANG Oh.

　　(Beat.)

This one . . . evening. That is to say, I *woke* . . . this one evening and wandered through the suite of rooms I shared with three other men. I was phantomy—I have acute night vision and—was lighter then—and was—I think—invisible to them—and I visited their—rooms—by which I mean their *bed*chambers—like—less than a breeze—and was not

noticed—and—one of the men was—pleasuring himself—
with two hands—Lord! that was impressive—and twisting
his head into his pillow—and crying out—his mother's
name—which was really—and the second of them was—
muttering obscenities softly into the dark—and the other—
slept—just—slept—breath in, breath out—and that
seemed—oddest of all—AND FOR THAT MOMENT—the
year that followed—I . . . thought that I wasn't . . . that I
might . . . I . . . paid attention at football games.

MILLY This story is about football games?

LANG Yes—deeply, deeply—about football games.

MILLY Would you like to take me to a football game?

(Pause.)

LANG (softly, staring at the keyboard) Well, yes, I suppose I
would . . .

MILLY Remember this night. Always remember this night.

LANG I don't have a choice.

MILLY Always remember this night.

   We danced.

   And I showed myself to you naked.

HOMER (appearing at doorway) And it's the first really
traditional Christmas we've had in years!

SCENE.

SCENE 4

Afternoon; HOMER *and* MILLY.

HOMER Welcome, Miss Ashmore, welcome, welcome, once again, to our home.

MILLY Where is your brother?

HOMER No, don't worry, it's just us. May I pour you some tea?

MILLY I want *nothing.*

HOMER *(pours her tea)* All right. You don't have to get huffy about—

MILLY Where could he have possibly gone without you?

HOMER An afternoon recital for ladies . . . in the *drawing* room of a *lady*—

MILLY How did you persuade him to do that?

HOMER I explained to him our finances—the condition of our finances— Sugar?

MILLY No.

HOMER *(drops four lumps into the cup)* I explained to him that the money they were offering was awfully good— I *reasoned* with him, I made him *see* that—

MILLY How did you get him to go?

HOMER I hit him.

(Beat.)

MILLY No. Really.

HOMER Well, you have to.

MILLY No. Really.

HOMER Well, it's Langley—

MILLY You didn't hit him—

HOMER He responds beautifully to physical violence—he always has—he becomes an angel of docility.

(Pause.)

MILLY That sort of thing doesn't happen here.

HOMER Doesn't it?

MILLY You know, Mr.— Homer, I have been trying in these last weeks to figure you out—to sift and winnow through your behavior to me—its violent, even perverse swings—and after careful consideration, I have come to the conclusion that you are extremely hard to read.

HOMER I shouldn't be—I'm an open book— Well, no, I'm more like an open *stack*, really—*Madame Bovary, c'est moi*—and also everybody else in the damn library—

MILLY You know, I'm not untrained in psychology—and—

HOMER I *know* this about you—you are utterly à la mode—that's your ferocious attraction—

MILLY What do you think of me, really?

  What do you think is the relationship among the three of us?

  How would you put it into words? How would you characterize it?

HOMER I would say . . . you're a silly little rich trollop who likes to tease our cocks.

MILLY Mr. Collyer!

HOMER Okay, let me try another one.

  You are . . . the spirit of the avant-garde incarnate . . . a quester after the new; it is by the efforts of you and your likes that the fallen, fractured, machine-wrecked world will once again be made whole.

MILLY . . . That's better.

HOMER I don't know. I think before I was closer to the mark.

MILLY I can leave—

HOMER But you won't.

Oh, listen: you're our *enzyme*. In your presence, reactions take place.

MILLY Why did you ask me here today?

HOMER I want to know your intentions toward my brother.

(*Pause. She laughs.*)

No, no, no. Answer.

MILLY How can I answer that?

Intentions are had *toward* women, not *by* them.

HOMER In this case, we'll have to make an exception.

MILLY It's not possible—

HOMER It simply has to be; you'll have to propose to him—

MILLY First of all, the presumption of you to assume I'm in any way interest—

HOMER Oh, don't fake—

MILLY —and even if I were—

HOMER Is there under all that—persiflage—a hard little throbbing little nugget of convention that really runs you?

(*Beat.*)

MILLY Will I have to sink to my knee?

HOMER Save that for after the wedding.

MILLY You're mad—

HOMER Well, how *else* is it going to happen? Do you expect me to start him in your direction in some way?

MILLY Well, maybe I do.

(*Beat.*)

HOMER Huh.

>I suppose I could *hit* him.

MILLY Flattering.

HOMER Oh, it isn't you—it's anything—anything—you can't get
>him to—that he *washes* regularly is only due to me—I am
>his—prime mover!—that's—

MILLY Then—does this mean—you *want* him to marry me?

HOMER I want the two of you to become engaged.

MILLY And to marry?

HOMER Oh no—I'll scuttle that.

MILLY You'll—

HOMER Or *fail* to—

MILLY Which?

HOMER There's no telling—that's the marvelous part!

MILLY Then—are we—allies, antagonists—what—

HOMER Antagonists, I hope. *(sincerely, like an offer of
>friendship)* I *want* us to be antagonists—

MILLY Do you hate me, Homer?

HOMER Not at all.

MILLY Then why do you act as though you do?

HOMER Because it makes for a better scene!

>*(Beat.)*

>Oh—look—you excite me—you—*excite* me—

MILLY I know—

HOMER I am my brother's accountant—do you know? I am:
>that.

>*(Beat.)*

>I was—when I was—a child—my mother—oh, let me
>start with her:

>My mother was a woman of taste.

MILLY *(satisfied smile)* I knew your mother would come into this.

HOMER If you only knew—the epic saga of my aunt Prudy's cheap lacquered vase—the infamy of its entry into our house—the diatribes my mother launched against it on a daily basis—and the way she managed—accidentally and in full view of my aunt—to sweep it off its pedestal and smash it into a thousand pieces!

MILLY So?

HOMER So?

Well.

I'm not sure . . .

That story has always seemed to have a point.

MILLY "I am my brother's accountant."

HOMER Yes!

When I was quite young, my mother said to me, "Homer, you are *for* your brother."

Can you imagine?

It was a kind of manifesto for my life; she was not a casual woman, there was an aura of fatality about the way she'd pour the *coffee*—so when she said—and I still so young—"You are *for* your brother"—I knew at once that my life would be devoted to dodging this proposition— Because you see—I wanted my own life.

MILLY Of course.

HOMER And had it . . .

I *do* have—I mean, the *past* . . . is *real* . . . it doesn't seem so, but it is. It is *true*.

MILLY I know.

I am the ruin of that truth.

(Beat.)

HOMER I'm sorry.

MILLY That's all right. I'm better . . . since Vienna . . . *(Beat.)*
　　　Tell me: How did you get from there to here? How did
　　　you end up tending to him after you'd made your escape?

HOMER Oh.
　　　Well.
　　　Fraternal love is a powerful—

MILLY No, really.

HOMER He was spending all our money.

MILLY I *knew* it was money!

HOMER All our property is held jointly, and it was made known
　　　to me that he was squandering it—and I came and took
　　　over.
　　　(Pause.)
　　　In addition, fraternal love is a powerful—

MILLY How *much* money is there?

HOMER Less and less.

MILLY Are you in danger of losing everything?

HOMER Oh, I hope so!

MILLY Homer.

HOMER I don't care what happens as long as something does.
　　　My brother's life is . . . one of . . . piecemeal intensities; I
　　　watch him.
　　　Some nights—weeknights—I watch him, right around
　　　seven P.M.—that poignant Booth Tarkington hour when
　　　people come home. Do you know, sometimes he cries? I can
　　　see him *weeping* for it—and I think as long as this still
　　　happens, then life is possible.
　　　But opportunity passes.
　　　I have *forgotten* how I got from there to here.

(Beat.)

MILLY Then I would be the mistress of this house.

HOMER Yes, sure, fine.

MILLY I would be in charge of the servants—

HOMER We don't have servants; every two weeks an old blind
woman comes in to spit on the dust—

MILLY There *will be* servants—

HOMER We can't keep them.

MILLY With me here, that won't be a problem. I'll be in charge.

HOMER Yes, fine.

MILLY Everything will have to change.

HOMER "Change"! The most thrilling of all words!

MILLY Now, about my money—

HOMER And there's the second most thrilling—

MILLY It would have to remain my money. I mean, the marriage
contract would have to be accompanied by another, rather
more realistic document that my lawyers will arrange. So
that in the event of anything at all happening, my property
would never be imperiled.

HOMER You do *love* my brother?

MILLY Passionately, romantically. I'll call on my lawyer tonight.

HOMER Fine—I love lawyers—I am one!
You won't . . . ?

MILLY Finish.

HOMER . . . love him too much, will you? Or understand him
too completely and let him know it? That wouldn't play well.

MILLY I understand him implicitly. He is an artist, therefore
turbulent, strange, possessed by passions unknown to the
common run of people. He needs to be cosseted, indulged,
and surreptitiously held in check.

HOMER Oh, good! Nothing to worry about.

MILLY *(to herself)* Marriage to him will be a great spite to my
   family.
      (Beat.)
      Well. What a lovely visit this has been!
HOMER So much accomplished.
MILLY Yes.

LANG *enters, ashen-faced and wobbly.*

LANG Homer—!
HOMER Lang—
LANG I can't—I can't—
HOMER What is it?
LANG Don't make me do that again—don't make me do that
   again—don't make me do that again—don't make me—
HOMER What happened?
LANG I can't tell you that—I can't tell you that—you *know* it's
   too much to tell— *(*HOMER *is holding him now, propping
   him up.)* Please don't make me do it again.
HOMER No, I won't—no—never—no, I won't—
LANG Hello, Milly.
MILLY Hello, Lang.
LANG Why is she here?
HOMER Oh. We were making some plans?
LANG *Plans!?* Do they include me?
HOMER Only to a negligible degree. Listen, why don't you go
   up now? Have a bath. I'll bring you something on a tray.
LANG Yes. Yes, all right.

HOMER *helps him out of the room. Left unsupported,* LANG
walks off, still wobbly.

MILLY Sweet to watch you walk him like that.

HOMER Fraternal love is a powerful thing.

MILLY I must to my lawyer before it's too late.

HOMER Yes. What time is it, anyway?

MILLY *(consults her watch)* Almost seven.

HOMER Seven.

MILLY Yes.

HOMER Seven P.M.

MILLY Yes.

HOMER And I'm in it! I'm in it!

SCENE.

SCENE 5

Morning. LANG *sits alone in morning coat and top hat.*
HOMER *enters.*

HOMER The musicians are getting antsy.

LANG Oh.

HOMER They seem to have a subsequent engagement and
would like to get under way—is there anything you would
like to tell them? Any advice or—

LANG Are they going to play?

HOMER Well, of course.

LANG Are they, in fact, *planning* to play?

HOMER That would complete the bargain, yes.

LANG They're going to play the Wedding Knell.

(Beat.)

HOMER Technically, it's a *march*.

LANG That's my least favorite kind of music.

HOMER Be that as it may—

LANG I abominate marches. If I had the money—and the
wherewithal—to order an assassination—my target would
be John Philip Sousa—

HOMER Lang—

LANG John Philip Sousa—I would eradicate John Philip
Sousa—if I were known—because it seems everyone must

be known for something—as the man who killed John Philip Sousa, it would be *fine*.

HOMER Let me look at you.

LANG Why?

HOMER I'm sure something on your person needs fixing.
    (looks) Yes. *(fiddles with* LANG's *tie)* Did you bathe today?

LANG I did.

HOMER Proud of you.

LANG You're choking me.

HOMER That's how you know it's fitting—

LANG Homer—

HOMER Yes?

LANG Will things—start to—*happen* now—I mean—

HOMER You have nothing to worry about.

MILLY *enters in a wedding gown.*

MILLY I think we may have Nyack!

She exits.

LANG What was that?

HOMER Your bride.

LANG What was she saying about Nyack?

HOMER I don't know.

LANG How do you—how does one *have* Nyack? I don't understand.

HOMER I don't know.

LANG Then what *good* are you?

HOMER I'm—

LANG What good are you?

HOMER Lang—

LANG You know I count on you for spurious explanations of enigmatic conditions; what *good* are you if you fail even at *that*?

MILLY *pops back in.*

MILLY Or, if not, Dobbs Ferry!

She pops out.

HOMER That's bad luck.
      To see your bride before the wedding.

LANG I didn't look.

HOMER Are you sure?

LANG Why would I look? She's not interesting.

HOMER . . . Good.

LANG . . . What a moron you are.

HOMER Why?

LANG I don't know—I don't know—God knows it doesn't run in the family—

HOMER You're being vehement—

LANG Your superstitions—and your—enchantment with irony—and your terrible, terrible taste—what a moron, what a moron!

HOMER This is *nerves* . . .

LANG Why am I—forced—to be in cahoots—with such a sentimental—dunce?—

HOMER You're nervous—

LANG *God!*

HOMER Nerves, nerves, nerves!

LANG GOD!
(Beat.)
HOMER Nerves.

MILLY *enters.*

MILLY Or Croton-on-Hudson.
(She starts out.)
HOMER HALT!
>   (She stops.)
>   What in the hell are you *talking* about?
MILLY Oh, dear, how funny!
>   I'm negotiating our wedding present.
LANG We're being given a *town*?
MILLY Darling, an estate.
LANG What do you mean?
MILLY It's self-evident—
LANG Homer, ask her what she means?
HOMER What do you mean?
MILLY An estate! Grounds, houses, horses, fountains—an
>   *estate*.
LANG This is our home.
HOMER This *is* your home.
MILLY Yes, yes, of course. Now, here's the thing: Nyack, you
>   see the Hudson year-round, where Croton-on-Hudson, you
>   only see the Hudson in winter, when the trees are bare.
>   Dobbs Ferry, you never see the Hudson at all, but it's the
>   size of Madison Square Garden. I think we have our *choice*,
>   you see, because I'm using blackmail.
LANG Blackmail?
MILLY In my situation, it's tremendously effective.

LANG Milly.

MILLY *(enters his arms)* Oh, darling, we have a lifetime of extortions before us. Is your hair really going to be doing that *at the* altar?

LANG This . . . is my home.

MILLY Of *course* it is.

LANG This . . . is my . . . no, you don't understand . . . this is my *home*—

MILLY And this will always *be* your home—*our* home.

Always. The other place will be just where we *stay*. On days of the week.

(Beat.)

LANG's *mouth opens in a kind of silent scream.* HOMER *goes to him, holds his head.*

LANG Homer—

HOMER Nothing will happen you don't want to happen.

LANG Homer—

HOMER I'm *here.*

LANG Homer—

HOMER Eternally. Eternally.

（LANG *visibly calms down.*）

（to MILLY）Would you say something to your father for me?

MILLY Yes, of course, what?

HOMER "I'll take it in cash, Daddy."

(Beat.)

MILLY We'll arrange for *something.*

She exits.

HOMER There.

LANG You *are* a fixer.

HOMER Yes.

LANG There is *that* about you.

HOMER There is.

LANG Yes.

(Beat.)

HOMER You're getting married.

LANG Yes.

HOMER In minutes.

LANG Yes. How long do you expect the ceremony will take?

HOMER I don't know—half an hour?

LANG Hm. Then I suppose that will give me plenty of time to spend with my *stamps*—

HOMER —to spend with—

LANG —before I fall asleep—I'll need seven or eight hours—it won't go longer than half an hour, do you—

HOMER Lang.

LANG . . . Yes.

HOMER This is your *wedding* day.

LANG In your mind, I suppose it is—

HOMER Shouldn't you tell me that you love me?

(Beat.)

LANG Why?

HOMER Because it's an occasion.

(Beat.)

LANG So?

HOMER Just, please . . . do.

(Pause.)

LANG I love you.

HOMER Thank you, Lang. And I—

LANG Yes, you're very right, I must try to remember that. I must make a mental note to tell you from time to time what it is you want to hear so you won't walk out on me and force me to learn to pay the bills by myself.

HOMER . . . Lang—

LANG Although I suppose now, with Milly . . .

Pause.
The quartet starts playing "The wedding march."

LANG A-A-A-A-A-A-A-A-A-A!!!!!!

HOMER All right—calm down—I'll stop them—!

He goes out.
LANG *goes to the piano and plays the opening notes of "The wedding march" slowly.*
After a moment, MILLY *comes in.*

MILLY Those idiot musicians—they've leapt their cue! Absolutely no sense of drama . . .

(LANG *stops playing, looks at her.*)

Oh dear, what a day. This *room* really *is* a mess . . .

LANG I don't think so . . .

MILLY Look at it—it's a *pig*sty! What if someone were to wander in from the party? Where's the wastepaper basket?

LANG We don't have a wastepaper basket.

MILLY What do you mean you don't have a wastepaper basket? Everybody has—

LANG I don't believe in wastepaper.

MILLY You— Well, that's absurd. That's idiotic. You can not believe in God, or something like that, but you *have* to believe in wastepaper. Wastepaper can be empirically proven. Now, where do you collect your trash?

LANG . . . I don't know.

MILLY Oh! You are in for such a renovation! Well, we're just going to have to kick this stuff under the furniture and hope against *hope* that nobody looks—

(She starts gathering and hiding.)

LANG Stop . . .

Stop . . .

Stop! Not that!

MILLY What?

LANG *That!*

MILLY . . . This? This is a . . . piece of string! It's come loose from a pull cord—

LANG Don't manhandle it like that—

MILLY Manhandle— Oh, look, look, I don't have time— We have to get married—but our first act as man and wife is going to be to *burn* this little piece of nothing. Now, slick down your hair, puff out your chest, and *march*, my angel; it's *time*.

LANG *(fondles the string)* I first saw this when I was in my crib—

MILLY What? That? Oh, please—

LANG I looked up—and saw it—it was—dazzlingly colored— nothing is ever lost on me, nothing ever leaves—it was the first thing of its kind I'd seen—and though I didn't know about words yet, I wanted desperately to name it—

MILLY Why not let's call it "string" and *get on* with this?

LANG I remember the desperation—

MILLY Oh, God.

LANG —and I remember reaching—Mother was breaking the
    hated vase, that would one day be legend—the nurse came
    at me as an apron—vast, white, starched—and some sweet,
    curdled smell entered the room—

MILLY Langley!

LANG —there were tears off to the left—a glittering of
    porcelain below—a spoon with the sweet white was thrust
    into my mouth—and piano notes played in the next room—
    and everything was entirely itself, and all at the same time.

MILLY They're just going to keep playing that monotonous
    tune until we show up, so I think we should think about
    showing up.

LANG So you see—

MILLY I mean, Lord! I have never known anyone to wander into
    parentheses with the zeal that you—

LANG So you see, the thing is—

MILLY All right, then, I'll go first. Upending all tradition!

LANG So you see, the thing is, I can't possibly marry you.
    (She turns.)
    Not possibly.

FADE.

❋ ACT TWO ❋

SCENE 1

HOMER *sits drinking.*

HOMER *(to no one)* And what happened next was . . . truly
remarkable.

   We . . .

   And what happened next will startle you.

   There was a . . .

   And what happened next was, everyone dashed about in
uproarious confusion; tears and cries and . . .

   And what happened next was . . .

   Ah! Well, then, you know that part, good . . .

   So.

   Ever since. Ah well.

   Diminishment, diminishment, fatigue. I . . .

   Do you know, there was a Frenchman, long ago, who
wrote a learned treatise about a lemon peel, which ran to
several volumes. I might get Lang started on something like
that. If it weren't for his near-total illiteracy. His hostility to
books. And his categorical rejection of categorical thought.

   If not for those small obstacles, we might get . . . a second
learned treatise on a lemon peel.

   . . . But no, he's too involved, anyway, with his *days*, his
ambit—haunting the streets, meditating or foraging, bearing

back all this exquisite . . . decor. Have you ever *seen* such extraor— Have you ever seen such an eclec—

Oh! What I love about our life is its originality, its revolutionary qualities, its improvisatory nature. I *love* that . . . about this . . .

I used to love—on bad days—I used to love—on days when I'd stayed indoors and weltered in my . . . freedoms . . . I used to love to walk around the block.

Simply that.

It was like coffee, the way everything woke up for me, all possible and kindly—the air—fresh or foul, but *there*—

Of course, can't do that much anymore, no, no, not much. Not since they started stoning us. Well: *pebbling* us, the neighborhood children, but still: sanctioned by their parents, even encouraged, I'd warrant.

That's unpleasant, you know. To be hit by rocks for no good reason. For no reason at all. Well. They have their reasons, I suppose . . . Things come flying through the window. No *sanctum sanctorum*, this. Things come flying.

The days all have a dingy brown cast to them. I miss . . . everything.

But I don't complain. You'll like that about me. I'm cheerful. I'm stoical. I cook. And I try to force a rhythm on the day. Which, in the absence of sunlight and sleep, is *quite* a job of work. To take a great undifferentiated wash of time and hack it into seasons. Less resourceful men couldn't . . . Less resourceful men wouldn't be able to . . .

Less resourceful men.

A clock tolls seven.
HOMER *shuts his eyes.*

Later. HOMER *sets the table for dinner.*
LANG *enters.*

LANG Homer!

HOMER Good evening, Lang.

LANG I'm back.

HOMER Yes, I see. I'm *happy* about that.

LANG It was lovely.

HOMER What was?

LANG All of it. The day.

HOMER Oh, did they miss?

LANG Yes, um, well, mostly.

HOMER I'm glad.

LANG And even when they—hit—I didn't pass out—or get sick—

HOMER That *was* a good day—

LANG Yes—did you cook?

HOMER Yes.

LANG What?

HOMER A stew.

LANG Good—I'm hungry.

HOMER Well, there's plenty.

LANG Good, I'm hungry.

HOMER Well, there's plenty.

LANG I was in the park.

HOMER Ah.

LANG All day . . .

HOMER Mm-hm.

LANG It was something.

HOMER Good. Wash your hands.

LANG Don't you want to hear about it?

HOMER Not at all. Wash up.

LANG Homer—

HOMER Or I won't feed you. I won't feed you if you have dirty
hands—

LANG My hands are clean—

HOMER Your hands are never clean—

LANG They *are*—antiseptic—

HOMER Your hands are filthy as a coal miner's.

LANG Spotless—

HOMER People see your hands, they think you're Welsh—

LANG Why won't you listen to me?

HOMER Because I know the sorts of things you have to say,
and I don't want to hear them—

LANG You—think you do—

HOMER I'm sure all you have to tell me is the story of a leaf or
something—

LANG Oh.

HOMER And I don't feel like attending to the story of a leaf
right now, Lang, I simply don't. I don't want to hear about its
texture or its striping or its shape or its rare visual appeal or
what you thought to call it. I'd rather listen to a narration of
some ancient Roman battle, or just sit in stony silence
eating stew, so wash your filthy hands, please, and let's get
on with our meal.

LANG It was an—extraordinary leaf—

HOMER I have no doubt—

LANG It was—truly—

HOMER A *god* among leaves—I'm sure—

LANG I—thought something before—

HOMER Oh, I *am* sorry—

LANG Don't be that way—

HOMER I'm not being any way—

LANG Snide—in that way—

HOMER I'm not— It's simply that I know how keenly you dislike ideas—

LANG I—

HOMER —generalities—abstractions—

LANG I—

HOMER —anything without an odor—I know because when I read to you—

LANG Homer—

HOMER —when I *would* read to you, that is, from Whitman and Thoreau and Emerson, I remember you so deeply approved their trances and deplored their having written them down.

LANG Nevertheless, there are—one or two principles—I mean—*some* things need to be—put into words—creeds or methods—or. *Or.*

HOMER Ah.

LANG And it occurred to me—

HOMER —as you gazed at this leaf—

LANG I am ignoring your *tone*—

HOMER Why not?

LANG It occurred to me that everything that *is* . . . is *fine*.

HOMER Was this before or after being pelted with rocks?

LANG After.

HOMER Well, then, it's earned. *(inspects* LANG's *hands)* Ugh. Wash.

LANG It's not as if your stew were worth the tribute of clean hands, you know—

HOMER Nevertheless.

LANG Lately it's been—viler and viler—I think you put the wrong ingredients in.

HOMER Nonsense.

LANG Yes—you pluck the wrong ingredients from the shelf— once I tasted library paste in the goulash—you've become—

HOMER That's ridiculous—

LANG —terribly careless—unless—

HOMER Possibly a cleaning fluid, never library—

LANG Unless you're trying to do away with me.

(Beat.)

HOMER What kind of tree still has its leaves in December?

LANG What?

HOMER I say: What kind of tree still has its leaves in December?

LANG An evergreen, of course.

HOMER Douglas fir?

LANG My name for it is—

HOMER So then what you were studying so diligently, all the day long, wasn't even really a *leaf* at all but more a kind of *spindle*?

LANG My name for it is—

HOMER Good Lord, you've been staring all day at a needle!

LANG My name for it is . . .

(HOMER is dishing out food.)

HOMER Well, *what*?

LANG Oh. I've forgotten.

HOMER Well, that's fine, then, isn't it? It means you can go back tomorrow and do exactly the same thing.

LANG Yes.

HOMER It means you can go back tomorrow and find exactly

the same leaf—oh dear, I hope you *tagged* it—you can go
back tomorrow and find the same leaf and *stare* at it again,
and *name* it, and forget it—

LANG I'm still young—

HOMER Sisyphus had the *best* life, didn't he?

LANG Yes.

HOMER He got up in the morning, he had something to do—!

LANG God, this is swill!

    Are you out to poison me?

(Beat.)

HOMER Try the wine.

LANG Homer—

HOMER I was thinking, Lang, just before, just today, while on
my *rounds*, you know—

LANG Homer—

HOMER —out to the butcher for the stew meat, to the dry-
goods store for twine, you know the route I go, daily,
dodging rocks—

LANG Yes—

HOMER Like marketing in the Crimea—

LANG Yes—

HOMER —and I was thinking— Oh no, but I don't want to hurt
your feelings.

(Beat.)

LANG What . . . were you thinking?

HOMER I couldn't.

LANG You're going to.

HOMER No, it's not—

LANG Homer, please—

HOMER I was thinking you've become almost ordinary.

LANG . . . I am?

HOMER Well—I mean—before, we thought—didn't we?—with the piano—that little bubble of talent that came and burst— we thought, here may be someone truly *strange*—

LANG I never—

HOMER Authentically *weird*—with all your *ways*—

LANG I never placed—any stock in that—

HOMER —and for a while, this weirdness seemed— Why aren't you eating?—

LANG Poison.

HOMER It seemed worthy of sustenance—

LANG I live my life the way I—

HOMER —but lately you more and more resemble—*won't* you try the wine?—you more and more resemble—

LANG Vintage strychnine, is it?

HOMER —just a garden-variety neurotic—

LANG Hm.

HOMER Just like all the other phobics and inverts and paranoiacs and what have you that modern life presents in such dazzling array—all the frail, frail people with their iron imperatives: "Oh, I mustn't sit *here*, I must sit *there*; I can't wash dishes, I'm afraid of *foam*; I couldn't possibly *work*, I have a terror of *energy*"—they're everywhere, it seems: the People Who Simply *Can't*. And they have a single thing in common: they always get their own way.

LANG I'm utterly renouncing you and food!

HOMER They always get their way. Do you know, I think I'll become a boring neurotic myself—I'm going to develop an imperative! I MUST BE SERVED! There! What do you think?

LANG Homer—

HOMER Only who will be *my* servant? *(silence; with some disgust)* I'm not out to kill you, you stupid sprat, I'm just an awful cook.

LANG You didn't used to be.

HOMER It's what comes from living alone.

LANG You live with me.

HOMER Yes. With you.

And cuspidors, crushed pince-nez, checkbooks from defunct accounts, pieces of a smashed demi-lunette, plumbing parts, rusted roasting pans, baseballs, spoons, pickling spices—

(A lacrosse stick comes hurtling through the window.)

LANG *(goes to it delightedly)* And a lacrosse stick!

(He picks it up delicately, with love.)

HOMER A lacrosse stick!

Look at this place! Will you—*look* at this place?

LANG That's all I ever do.

HOMER How can anyone care for all this junk?

LANG How long and lovely it is—all cracked and burnished— and the basket all snarled—

HOMER Why do you care?

LANG It's *lovely*, Homer; it's sacred.

HOMER Sacred! You're an atheist!

LANG God isn't the source of what's sacred.

HOMER Then what is?

LANG Things in themselves.

HOMER All this junk—I promise you—one day I will toss out all this junk—

LANG And I'll go, too.

HOMER Why?

LANG It's what I love.

HOMER How?

LANG Easily.

HOMER I try to imagine it—in myself—I try to imagine
myself—shunning people—and loving duffel—

LANG How can there be love without duffel?

HOMER "How can there be . . . love without—"
Only it's not even duffel. Duffel can be gathered up, you
can travel with it, you can *take* it *with* you—

LANG It is with me, Homer. All the time. Every scrap.

HOMER . . . No . . . I can't do it. It doesn't work on me. I can't
make myself resemble you.

LANG We're not metaphors for each other, Homer—

HOMER You're the only thing there is for me to know—and I'm
failing at it—utterly—and I can't bear it—

LANG Everything that is, is fine.

HOMER Not for me.

(Beat.)

LANG *(a concession)* You can throw out the newspapers.

HOMER Langley?

LANG Yes, Homer?

HOMER The newspapers are mine!

LANG You don't even read them anymore.

HOMER But they're *mine*!

LANG Useless things with ugly names.

HOMER *(a litany)* The *Times*, the *World*, the *Record*, the
Ledger—

LANG Ugh!

HOMER The *Times* . . . the *World* . . . the *Record* . . . the
Ledger.
I can't bear it!

LANG *(mollifying)* Everything that is, is—

HOMER Oh, will you shut up with that inane little bromide!

LANG You just need to relax. You need to calm down.
  This *is* our life.

HOMER Maybe I *ought* to kill you.

LANG Well. That will have to be *your* decision.
  (from outside, the sound of Christmas carolers)
  Oh! Is it Christmas?

HOMER . . . Yes . . .

LANG I wonder what they're going to throw at us!

HOMER No . . . these don't seem that sort . . .

LANG Oh. Must be strangers.

HOMER Yes.

LANG Excruciating singing.

HOMER Yes. So pretty.

LANG The seventh boy from the left is flat—

HOMER It reminds me of—

LANG A solid eighth tone flat—it's torture—

HOMER —nothing. It reminds me of nothing.

HOMER *listens, wistful.* LANG *puts his hands over his ears.*
The carolers finish, move on.

LANG That was hell.

HOMER Lang? I'm getting married.

(Pause.)

LANG Ha-ha.

HOMER No, I mean it.

LANG Ha.

HOMER No, I mean it.

LANG You lie—

HOMER I'm going to get married . . . awfully soon—

LANG You lie in your very own *house*—

HOMER You must prepare for it—

LANG Yes. All right.

HOMER You must make some attempt to master the minutiae of your own existence, because I'll be too busy—

LANG —of course—

HOMER —copulating and so forth—to see to it—that you don't—reek or starve or—

LANG Yes, fine—

HOMER —impale yourself on something *sacred*—

LANG Yes, of course, Homer—

HOMER Because in a minute, I'll be—blind—and toothless— and no longer eligible, and I can't—pass up the last chance I may ever have to . . . to . . . to . . .

LANG I understand.

He goes back to the lacrosse stick.
Pause.

HOMER *(a stifled cry)* Lang!

   *(*LANG *looks at him.)*

   Please . . . read to me.

LANG I hate that job.

HOMER Please.

LANG Why can't you read to yourself?

HOMER I'm afraid . . . we'll stop talking. I'm afraid the evening will go silent . . . Please.

*(*LANG *pulls a book off the shelf.)*

LANG *(reads)*

"It was utterly wonderful to me to find that I could go so heartily and headily mad; for you know I had been priding myself on my peculiar sanity!"

(He tosses the book over his shoulder, then picks up another book.)

"In recording everything that the Roman people has experienced in successive wars up to the time of writing I have followed this plan—that of arranging all the events described as far as possible in accordance with the actual times and places."

(He picks up another book.)

"To regard all things and principles of things as inconstant modes or fashions has more and more become the tendency of modern thought."

(again)

"My purpose is to consider if, in political society, there can be any legitimate and sure principle of government, taking men as they are and laws as they might be."

(again)

"If this should be the case with you, you will eternally curse this day, and will curse the day that ever you was born, to see such a season of the pouring out of God's spirit, and will wish that you had died and gone to hell before you had seen it."

(He looks up.)

Is that enough?

(Pause.)

HOMER *(quiet despair)* Yes.

LANG Yay!

(He returns to the lacrosse stick.)

Time for this!
Time for everything . . .
Homer?

HOMER . . . Yes?

LANG I love our life.

(Pause.)

HOMER Oh.

SCENE.

SCENE 2

*Middle of the night. The doors to the front hall open. Light
streams in from outdoors. Loud, slow knocking at the front
door.* HOMER *appears and peeks around the stairs.*

HOMER *(whispers)* . . . Yes?
  (more knocking, slightly louder)
  Yes?
VOICE Please . . .
HOMER Go away.
VOICE Please let me in.
HOMER . . . Go away. This is not where you mean to be.
VOICE Please help me.
HOMER Ah.
  Go away now.
VOICE Please help me. It's Christmas.
HOMER Yes. Merry Christmas. Please leave.
  (knocking again)
  Please don't do that!
VOICE I should like to come in . . .
HOMER Oh no.
  Maybe once upon a time . . .
  (knocking)
  Please stop pounding!

VOICE I will.

Knock-knock.

HOMER Who's there—oh dear God!

Please . . . go. We are in bad enough odor with the
neighbors as it is.

VOICE I'm freezing. I don't mean you any harm.

A corpse in your doorway will look much worse than a
wraith in your parlor.

HOMER . . . Oh . . . Oh.

*(He starts toward the door, trips over things, slides a
ways.)*

VOICE Are you all right?

HOMER I'm . . .

No!

. . . Yes. I'm fine.

VOICE Please let me in.

HOMER Yes, I will.

He gets up, crosses to the door, and unlatches it. A WOMAN
enters in a hooded cape, ashen, sickly.

Who are you?

WOMAN The Ghost of Christmas Past, of course.

HOMER Why have you come here?

WOMAN I've always found this house inviting.

(Beat.)

HOMER I don't understand.

WOMAN Is there someplace I can warm my hands?

HOMER No. We can't go lighting a fire at this hour. Besides,
they're dangerous these days, it's a houseful of kindling,

nothing but, so no, I'm afraid there's no place a person can
warm his or her hands at all—
  (She shivers.)
  Yes. In mine.
(He takes her hands.)
WOMAN Thank you.
  It's good to see you again.
HOMER I'm . . . terribly—confused—
  You seem to— Who are—
  (He stares at her.)
  Milly.
MILLY Oh.
  So I've changed *that* much.
HOMER Milly. What's happened to you?
MILLY *(breaking down)* Everything; everything has happened
  to me!

SCENE.

SCENE 3

A few minutes later. There is a fire. MILLY *sits, eating stew.*

MILLY This is lovely.

HOMER You're starving.

MILLY I am, but this is lovely.

HOMER It doesn't strike you as odd?

MILLY No. Should it?

HOMER Well, one pulls anything from the shelf—

MILLY It's lovely—

HOMER —without paying attention—

MILLY Now that you mention it, there is something slightly
off—

HOMER Library paste?

MILLY No, I *like* the library paste; could it be cinnamon?

HOMER Yes. Who knows?

I may have been reaching for a slim pencil, pulled down
the nearest thing—left it for days—threw it in the stew.

MILLY Lovely. Just lovely.

(She eats, sighs.)

It's getting nice and toasty in here.

(She takes off her hood; her hair is steel gray.)

HOMER Oh dear God . . .

MILLY What?

HOMER There's something on your head.

MILLY Only my hair.

HOMER Is that your hair?

MILLY It's turned, yes . . . Please don't stare at—

HOMER I'm trying to make it out.

MILLY It's white, that's all. You've seen white hair before.

HOMER Not on a child.

MILLY . . . I'm not a child anymore.

HOMER What's happened to you?

MILLY Not yet, in a moment, not just yet.

    (trying for brightness)

    I've looked—I haven't seen—I've looked on the billboards;
Langley doesn't seem to be performing anywhere—

HOMER . . . That's stopped.

MILLY But why?

HOMER He's no longer employable. His tempi became too slow.

MILLY I suppose that's how he heard the music.

HOMER No.

    He couldn't bear to let the notes go.

    Look at the fire. Wouldn't it be lovely if it took the whole room? Wouldn't it be lovely if it spread and spread and took us all?

    You can never see things becoming impossible. If only you knew beforehand the forces are . . . invisible . . . that bring you to a stop, you might be able to prepare . . . One day you can't muster the will to cross the room. Open spaces . . . impassable . . . everywhere . . . Who saw it coming?

    Tell me what happened to you.

    Tell me what happened next.

MILLY Not yet—

HOMER *Please*. I need to know what happened next.

(Pause.)

MILLY It started on the trip back from the wedding-that-never-was.

> We didn't speak, my mother, my father, and I.
>
> All I could think of was fault—and the fault was mine.
>
> I had played this part badly.
>
> I couldn't endure who I was: my parents' daughter.
>
> This rich ninny, this fool.
>
> I took to my bed and would not come out.
>
> Then through the shafts and vents of the house, I heard
>
> my parents conspire.
>
> Inventing a story to explain away the debacle
>
> uptown.

HOMER *(with barely suppressed eagerness)* What—what was the story?

MILLY Illness, they said—the illness of the Collyers—and unspeakable deeds revealed in the nick of time—

HOMER If only.

MILLY I lay silent.

> For days in bed.
>
> And soon fell ill.
>
> At first I thought it was my mind, my mind attacking my body—that happens sometimes—psychosomatism, it's called—but it wasn't that.

HOMER What was it?

(Pause.)

MILLY I was pregnant, Homer.

HOMER What!

Did something happen I didn't supervise?

MILLY It wasn't your brother—

HOMER Did you *cheat*?

MILLY No.

HOMER A second Annunciation—?

MILLY It happened at home.

(Pause.)

HOMER Oh dear God. Dear God.

MILLY No longer dear to me.

HOMER What happened . . . to the child?

MILLY It was removed. Thank God.

HOMER . . . I am sorry.

MILLY Then I started to speak.

HOMER To speak?

MILLY In people's houses, I took to muttering.

The truth! The truth! This is how things are!

I became the well-dressed madwoman gibbering on the Queen Anne chair.

Until . . . my parents . . . put me away.

HOMER Back to Vienna?

MILLY A public facility.

HOMER No!

MILLY For punishment. For warning.

A place of bars and straitjackets and all-night howling.

That's how it . . . how my hair . . .

And there I almost *did* go mad.

But not quite.

And when I was let out—when it was thought that I was scared enough and scandalized enough to be released without causing harm . . . I resumed my story:

"My *father* did this—he's not the man you think you know!"

  And then I was disowned.

HOMER This has *twists.*

MILLY Homer, these things *happened*—

HOMER Yes—

MILLY To me—

HOMER Yes—

MILLY —and were *dreadful*—don't *want* them.

HOMER No—no—I don't want the *events*—but please give me more of the *story.*

(Beat.)

MILLY My father paid a man—a scurrilous man—to testify that many years before, he had . . . lain with my mother. That he, my father, was not my father—this other man—this twisted, terrible man—that's where the madness came from—that's where all the error started.

  My mother—disgraced—divorced.

  I disowned.

  My father free of scandal. Of taint.

  A new man.

HOMER And since then . . . ?

MILLY I've found the streets to be friendlier than the houses on them.

*(*HOMER *sits back, satisfied.)*

HOMER That tale—what a *corker*!

  (He takes her hand.)

  I'm so terribly sorry.

She nods, keeps her hand in his, cries. It builds. He holds her.

LANG *enters.*

LANG Noises . . . noises . . . nois— What's *happen—*
　　(*He sees the two of them.*)
　　. . . No *no* NO!
(*And he faints.*)

SCENE.

SCENE 4

The next morning. LANG *alone, brooding.* HOMER *enters with food on a tray and makes a stumbling path to a table, where he lays out settings.*

HOMER Ah, you've awakened!

LANG Homer . . . ?

HOMER Last night I wasn't sure you would.

LANG Homer . . . ?

HOMER Suddenly passing out in this place—I wouldn't advise it. All sorts of objects to nick yourself on, to cut and scrape yourself on, to concuss you: weaponry, everywhere weaponry—sharp edges, blunt weights. Tread carefully.

LANG Did I pass out?

HOMER Out! Out! The discovery! The cry! Then *down* like a plumb line, it was—

LANG The discovery—

HOMER —entertaining. Oh. Yes.

LANG What did I discover?

HOMER *(to himself but a tease)* Hmmm.

LANG . . . Homer, I think I saw a ghost last night.

HOMER A ghost?

LANG Yes.

HOMER A *ghost*?

LANG Yes!

HOMER You mean an actual, corporeal, flesh-and-blood *specter*?

LANG I thought I saw that girl.

HOMER Girl . . . girl . . . I can't think who you mean . . .

LANG Homer!

HOMER I can't think *who*—

LANG From before . . .

HOMER *. . . From when before?*

LANG From the wedding.

HOMER Oh.

Which girl from the wedding?

LANG The bride.

HOMER Oh! Milly.

LANG . . . Yes.

HOMER Your affianced.

LANG *(with some distaste)* . . . Yes.

HOMER You thought you saw Milly?

LANG Her ghost.

HOMER Hmm.

LANG It was all so sudden.

HOMER I see.

LANG She was different . . . yet the same. *I don't see how different things can be the same!* But she was. Her hair was . . .

HOMER Ye-e-es?

LANG . . . silvered in the moonlight—

HOMER *(smiles to himself)* Oh, in the moonlight—

LANG Yes—in the moonlight—and she was dead—

HOMER Well: a *ghost*.

LANG All her living stuff was gone—bone and blood—but the light transfused her—

HOMER Oh!

LANG —exposed her—

HOMER Ah-huh—

LANG —separated her particles—

HOMER Oh dear-dear-dear-dear-*dear*-dear-dear—

LANG She was herself with *time* added.

    (Pause.)

    Why did she come?

HOMER . . . Well, it was a dream, *ob*viously.

LANG Was it a dream?

HOMER What else?

    Wash for breakfast.

LANG I can stay dirty; the breakfast won't mind.

    It was a dream? Do you promise?

HOMER Yes.

LANG Do you swear?

HOMER Yes!

LANG Do you promise you swear?

HOMER I swear on the soul of . . . *(lifts from table)* this butter knife: that was only a dream.

LANG Thank you.

    WHY HAVE YOU SET THREE PLACES?

HOMER Hmm?

LANG *Three* places—*three* places—

HOMER Oh. Have I set three places?

LANG Yes!

(Beat.)

HOMER Well . . . you never know when somebody might
   drop by.

LANG *Here?*

HOMER One must always be prepared—

LANG People don't "drop by" this place, Homer—

HOMER I read once . . . in a book of etiquette—that the
   successful host—well, hostess, actually—hm. Hm . . .
   Anyway, that the successful host must always have sufficient
   provender on hand for the odd unexpected visitor.

LANG It would have to be an extremely odd visitor in our
   case.

HOMER Yes—but you never know, do you?
      You never know.

LANG . . . Homer—

HOMER Things might change.

(Beat.)

LANG Homer—

HOMER *(overlaps)* Things might be changing as I speak.

LANG *(a plea) H*omer—

HOMER *As I speak.*

LANG Homer?

HOMER Yes, Lang?

LANG *Why are you setting places?*

HOMER Oh, dear.

LANG We don't *do* that here.

HOMER Stop whining.

LANG *What's going on?*

HOMER Nothing, Lang.
      As ever.

LANG Do you swear?

HOMER Of *course* I do.

    Everything is as it was.

MILLY *enters.*

MILLY Good morning.

LANG *(a scream)* A-A-A-A-A-A-A-A-A-A-A-A!

*He drops like a plumb line, closes his eyes, and opens them
again.*

HOMER Hmmm.

MILLY That again.

LANG Oh no.

    I'm still *here.* I'm still *awake.*

HOMER Isn't that the trouble: things are never the same,
    merely id*en*tical.

    (to MILLY*)* Did you sleep?

MILLY I did, finally.

LANG I'm *awake*—it's daylight—

HOMER Finally?

MILLY I had to adjust to comfort.

HOMER That room seemed comfortable to you?

MILLY It had walls.

HOMER Oh, so you were able to find the walls, were you?

LANG I'm very unhappy!

MILLY Yes—

HOMER *In*teresting—

MILLY I couldn't *see* them, mind you—

HOMER Oh no, no—

MILLY But I felt them—I mean to say, I could de*duce* their
  presence—

HOMER Oh, yes—

LANG I'm very *very* unhappy—

MILLY And a ceiling, too!

HOMER Yes, yes—we pride ourselves on supplying all the
  amenities—

MILLY *(looks around)* I should say! It's a veritable bazaar in
  here—how did you ever acquire such interesting
  miscellany?

HOMER This stuff, you mean?

  Gifts, mostly. From the neighbors.

LANG *How* did this *hap*pen?

MILLY Have you become popular with the neighbors?

HOMER With the neighbors who have *pitching* arms, we are.

MILLY Ah.

HOMER Things come winging through the broken glass—bricks
  and books and things—Lang takes charge of them.

MILLY In what sense "takes charge"?

HOMER You might well ask.

  Yes—objects enter—Lang doesn't reject them—he
  doesn't burn them or pulp them or return them—he curates
  them—

MILLY How nice.

HOMER Assesses their value—dwells—

LANG Answer me—

HOMER I mean that seriously—

LANG *Answer me*—

HOMER Others merely have homes—we truly have a *dwelling*
  place.

LANG YOU MUST LEAVE NOW!

(Pause.)

HOMER I think not.

LANG I *demand* it.

HOMER I *counter*mand it.

LANG This is my *home*!

HOMER Well, maybe it isn't.

> (Beat.)
>
> I *am*, after all, a lawyer.
>
> Maybe I've had you declared incompetent and taken control of your interests.

LANG You didn't.

HOMER I *might* have.

> Having you found incompetent wouldn't exactly be a Herculean feat. I mean: maybe I have.

LANG Homer—

HOMER And if I haven't, maybe I will.

LANG . . .

> I refuse this!

HOMER Ah!

LANG I will not be drawn into your . . . grubby . . . contingencies—

HOMER All right. Then sit up straight and eat your breakfast.

LANG Not while she's here, no! No! No!

HOMER *(explaining to her)* A tantrum.

LANG Besides, there isn't any.

HOMER What?

LANG Breakfast.

HOMER Where?

LANG On these plates.

HOMER Of course there is.

LANG There isn't.

HOMER Isn't there?

MILLY Actually, no.

(HOMER *squints at his plate.*)

HOMER I'd forget my head if I had my druthers.

There are biscuits, I'll fetch them.

(*He stumbles over stuff on his way to the sideboard.*)

MILLY Careful!

HOMER CAN'T THERE BE A STRAIGHT LINE BETWEEN
ONE POINT AND ANOTHER *SOMEWHERE* IN THIS
HOUSE?

LANG There's nothing but straight lines.

MILLY Are you all right?

LANG Very very short straight lines.

HOMER I am . . . thank you.

Thank you for asking.

MILLY Well, of course.

(HOMER *returns gingerly with a plate of biscuits.*)

HOMER I am unused to someone asking.

MILLY Of course.

LANG (*slams his hands on the table*) GET OUT!

HOMER Pay no attention to him.

Have a biscuit instead.

LANG It's probably poisoned.

HOMER I can assure you it's not poisoned; it just tastes that
way.

MILLY I don't mind.

LANG *Why have you come?*

MILLY Not to accuse you, you needn't worry about that.

LANG Accuse me? What could you accuse me of?

HOMER All sorts of things—breach of promise—!

LANG Breach of *promise*—?

HOMER It's done in these situations—it's even traditional—

LANG In bad literature—

HOMER Well, life is like that sometimes—

LANG In the books you used to read—

MILLY Used to?

LANG *Why have you come?*

MILLY This is as good a place as any to die.

(Beat.)

HOMER Better. Here the difference is so much less marked.

MILLY An easy passage . . . a slide . . .

HOMER You won't be dying.

MILLY Of course I will.

HOMER Not soon . . . not soon.

MILLY After everything that's happened . . . what else?

HOMER I'll take care of you.

You'll stay here.

(Beat.)

LANG N-O-O-O-O-O!

HOMER You'll stay here.

I'll tend to you.

MILLY This is no sort of place to convalesce—

HOMER Then I'll change it—I'll change the place.

LANG No no no no no!

HOMER I'll change it for you.

MILLY And what will I do for you?

HOMER You'll *be*.

You'll simply be.

MILLY That's not enough.

HOMER And you'll *read* to me!

LANG *I* do that!

HOMER Ineptly.

MILLY Read to you?

HOMER It's been so long since I've been with a book.

MILLY Why don't you read them by yourself?

HOMER I . . . long for the sound of another's voice.

MILLY Homer, are you blind?

(Long pause.)

HOMER Yes.

MILLY Oh my dear . . . my dear . . .

HOMER Not entirely, of course . . . not yet. Light still, and
shapes, and sometimes a good deal more. Now. Eventually,
there'll be nothing.

MILLY I'm so sorry.

LANG You're WHAT?

HOMER Thank you for noticing.

MILLY Dear Homer . . .

LANG You're *blind*?

MILLY *(realizing)* "Blind Homer"—oh God!

HOMER *(smiles)* I know—incredibly pat, isn't it?
    I find that comforting somehow. Life goes along—
happening or . . . not . . . chaotic . . . and then you're all at
once "Blind Homer"!—Literature in*sists* on itself—

MILLY A pattern—

HOMER An identity—

MILLY A solace.

HOMER Yes.

LANG I AM IN THIS ROOM!

HOMER And no one seems to care: funny, that.

LANG Why didn't you *tell* me?

HOMER I was hoping one day you might figure it out on your own. I thought one day I might become your object of contemplation.

LANG Homer.

HOMER *(to* MILLY*)* We'll build you up.

MILLY . . . Yes. Thank you.

HOMER And you'll continue, won't you, your researches on the street?

MILLY If that's what you'd like—

HOMER Going out and bringing back information—

MILLY I shall—

HOMER About what the women are wearing and the plays in the theaters and whether there's an international war or whatever . . .

MILLY We'll take care of each other.

HOMER *(sealing it)* Very good.

MILLY Do you know what I've often wondered?

HOMER What?

MILLY After the wedding-that-never-was . . .

HOMER Yes?

MILLY The game was called, the guests adjourned—what happened to all that food?

HOMER It's under here somewhere.

MILLY I might have to do a bit of straightening up, if you don't mind.

HOMER Fine with me.

LANG You can't let a woman in this house—

HOMER Oh, but I can . . .

MILLY And we'll have doctors!

HOMER All right.

LANG When women enter, *events* take place. They should have
    stopped making them after the first try—

HOMER Idiocy.

LANG It says so in the Bible!

MILLY Unless you finally did go broke. Did you finally—?

HOMER Oh no, there was never any danger of that.

MILLY But . . . you said . . .

HOMER That was just a way of moving things along.

LANG Homer, an adult woman cannot come and simply live in
    this house—it's an affront to all the decencies!

Pause. MILLY *and* HOMER *smile at what a bourgeois prig he is.*

HOMER Then I'll marry her.
    If she'll have me.

MILLY *(softly)* Homer—

(HOMER *gets down on bended knee.*)

HOMER Will you marry me, Miss Ashmore?

MILLY Of course.

LANG But— *I* was supposed to do that.

HOMER Too late.
    Oh, this will be fun!
    What did that German say—all history happens twice,
    first as tragedy, then as farce?
    We'll do it *twice* as farce.

LANG Homer—

HOMER *Listen, you:*

*And very quietly, he is more fierce, more threatening, than
we've ever heard him: a new tone entirely.*

This woman has come to us. She has entered our home. She is the tiny thing that has happened in our lives, our smidgen of plot, and I want more of it, do you understand?

This house is mine, you're just a boarder here. You had your chances, you had your time, that's *over*.

(Beat. He straightens up, dusts himself off.)

Now. I am going out, into the day, and seeing about our future.

Meanwhile, why doesn't somebody find a broom?

And with great dignity, he walks out, stumbling badly but defiantly on everything as he goes.

A moment.

MILLY We might have a fine little time, we three.

LANG There are poisons in this house—things you can sprinkle on food—

MILLY *(mildly chiding)* Lang.

LANG Beware.

(Pause.)

MILLY Well . . .

And she leaves the room. We see how very weak she is as she goes.

Well.

SCENE.

SCENE 5

Years have passed. More detritus has piled up. Thousands of newspapers. HOMER *sits alone, totally blind.*

HOMER *(to no one)* My brother's a special case.

You—you say to me: "You had an outdoor life once, why not coax him into the world?"

My brother makes an epic of a molecule—what would he do with the world? He must stay inside, and he must be cared for. I'm more ordinary, and so I tend to him.

How *dare* you talk of the world, anyway—so easy, so smug with it— No matter.

Whatever you say . . .

No matter what you say: *our life is better than yours.*

(An old clock comes flying through the window.)

Thanks for the contribution!

HOMER *cackles.*

HOMER *goes silent.*

LANG *enters.*

LANG I've had the most wonderful day!

HOMER Have you, Lang?

LANG Yes.

HOMER What did you do?

LANG I looked at a bud vase.

HOMER Oh, a bud vase!

LANG In the parlor window—

HOMER Upstairs—

LANG Yes, the upstairs parlor—

HOMER In that niche—

LANG Yes, in the niche—the day was so fine, so bright—

HOMER Ah.

LANG I chronicled it—

HOMER Chronicled, really? In any particular order?

LANG The history of sunlight through clear glass!

HOMER And did you write it down?

LANG I noted every permutation of light. I named shades that have been overlooked by the conventional spectrum. Do you like "dullish apricot"? Or how about "twilight raiment"?

HOMER Fancy.

LANG I went wild with the names, Homer—

HOMER Evidently—

LANG I was Adam before the inconvenience of Eve!

(Beat.)

HOMER Ah.

Silence. There's a desperation under this now, something resigned, withdrawn, about HOMER: *a terrible lack of energy that is answered in* LANG *by unspoken anxiety.*

LANG *(feebly)* And what did you do?
    (Silence.)
    Shall we have our walk?

HOMER I don't feel like it today—

LANG I'll take your arm—

HOMER Even so—

LANG I'll pilot you—

HOMER No—

LANG I'll try not to bump you into things—

HOMER No, thank you.

Thank you very much.

(Beat.)

LANG I won't narrate—

HOMER Even so—

LANG I won't draw you into culs-de-sac and pick up, say, that teakwood pillbox and tell you, for example, that its dimensions are three inches by two inches by three inches and that it's of teak, which is a wood deeper-toned than cherry but lighter than mahogany—

HOMER Lang—

LANG —and of medium-rough grain, a grain that rises in near-black striations—

HOMER Lang—

LANG —and that holding it lightly in your palm does nearly nothing to affect body temperature—

HOMER Please stop.

(Beat.)

LANG But I haven't finished.

HOMER Please stop.

LANG But I haven't finished.

HOMER Please.

With visible difficulty, LANG *refrains from continuing. Beat.*

LANG I really haven't finished, Homer.

HOMER Even so.

LANG But I really haven't—

HOMER All the same.

> (*Beat.* LANG, *forlorn, brightens.*)

LANG Oh, Homer! I completed the rigging!

HOMER The rigging?

LANG Yes.

> Oh, it was wonderful, I worked it out. All this gantrified rigging, all pulleys and trip wires—so if, say, a thief, an intruder, in*trudes*: DOWN it will come on him. I took all these *objects*—there were actually a few spare lying about the house—and got this netting—tons and tons will come down, killing the intruder, so we're safe.

HOMER Ah.

LANG (*with some force, a kind of bruised defiance*) We're safe.

HOMER . . . Ah.

(*Pause.*)

LANG The bud vase was . . . a miraculous—!

> (*Pause.*)

> Homer, have I wasted this day?

HOMER No, Lang, I'm the one who wastes the day.

> (*Pause.*)

> Lang—

LANG No, no, no, I'm going to read to you—

HOMER I don't want to be read to—

LANG Yes—the way you love—

HOMER Not today—not anymore—

LANG (*plucking books from shelves*) Yes—I'll even go in order, the way you like—

HOMER Not today, Lang—not anymore—

LANG *(with gritted teeth)* I'm *going* to do this for you—here's
a book! "In the beginning, God created"— Oh, we already
know how this one turns out— I'll get something else—

HOMER Lang, I'm going to die today.

(Pause.)

LANG N-O-O-O-O-O-O!

HOMER But I am. I am. No, quiet now.
You'll need to be taken care of—

LANG Don't tell me this—

HOMER I managed, when you were upstairs on retreat—with a
hairpin, I think—I managed to make a telephone call. To
someone I once knew, when there were people—someone
who can arrange for your care—for an attendant—someone
who can handle whatever money needs to be handled—

LANG DO NOT TALK TO ME ABOUT THE TELEPHONE! I
*PRO*TESTED THE TELEPHONE!

HOMER —and whatever *hygiene* needs to be attended to—

LANG I'M NOT HEARING THIS!

HOMER —I've written down his name and number, right here,
but of course I don't know if they can be read—

LANG Homer—

HOMER —so why not give it a look, hm?

LANG If you do this thing—

HOMER This is not a thing you do—

LANG I swear to you—

HOMER This is a thing that's done to you—

LANG I swear to you, I'll trip the wire—yes!—I'll trip the wire
myself and bring down—all this debris upon my head—I
promise you—it will be a suicide-by-things—!

HOMER And then we'll be a story after all.

(Beat.)

Now, here is the paper on which I've written—

LANG *(covers his ears, paces, stumbles around the place)*
No-no-no-no-no-no-no—

HOMER This fellow's name and number—can you read it?

(LANG lunges to the piano.)

LANG Homer, I'm going to restart my career!

HOMER I don't imagine so . . .

LANG I am—I am—you'll have to manage me—to order me
about—remember how you—loved to— Here, here—

*He starts playing, too fast for the tune to establish itself,
feverish.*

My technique hasn't slipped a bit—

HOMER What is this?

LANG Not a bit!

HOMER What are you—

LANG *(hums madly along)*

HOMER What are you playing?

LANG Da-da-duh-duh-duh—

HOMER Is this "The Minute Waltz"?

LANG Yes!

HOMER Why are you taking it so fast?

LANG Making up for lost time!
(And he stops abruptly.)
Oh, please don't.

HOMER It's not my *choice*, Lang.

LANG Don't do this now.

HOMER It will always be "now" . . .

LANG You can stop it—

HOMER It's happening.

All I can do is succumb.

(Outside, carolers sing.)

LANG Homer, is it Christmas *again*?

HOMER It seems so, Lang.

LANG As it was . . . this day . . . a year ago . . .

HOMER Yes, Lang.

LANG *(agonized)* There's such a thing as a year . . .

(seized by panic)

Oh God—oh God—oh God—

I have to—I need—I need to—there are *things* I need to *do*—rites and celebrations, ceremonies I need—to accomplish—schedules I need to—abide by—observances and—tasks—but what—what are they? Oh, what do people do who live in a row?

Homer!

I have to confess myself!

HOMER I think that's taking it a little far.

LANG Yes—yes—I have to confess myself to you if you insist on— I mean, if you're *going* to—

HOMER All right—all right—yes—all right—

LANG I have to—expiate my sins—

HOMER Oh dear, you are going whole hog, aren't you?

LANG You have to . . . absolve me of my . . . sins—

HOMER All right, Lang, all right.

LANG That girl . . . that girl who came here . . . that time . . .

HOMER . . . Milly.

LANG Yes, that woman—

When she died . . . like that . . .

HOMER Yes.

LANG I mean, when she *per*ished that way—

HOMER . . . Yes—

LANG On the eve of your wedding, on the bed with the quilt, the quilt that's made of 636 mismatched squares of—

HOMER *(moving him along)* Yes, Lang, yes . . . ?

LANG . . . *I* did it.

(Pause.)

HOMER She died of tuberculosis.

LANG I *wished* for it.

HOMER *(gently)* I know you did.

But she died of tuberculosis.

LANG No. She died of my wish.

(anguished)

Even a *wish* . . . .

(Beat; then simply.)

It's a mistake to start.

(Beat.)

HOMER *(extends the paper)* Can you read this?

LANG *(takes it, lets it fall unread in a heap)* . . . Yes.

HOMER And you will call?

LANG *What will I do?*

HOMER You'll call.

Someone will take care of you.

LANG It won't be the same.

HOMER It will be *exactly* the same.

A stranger will tend to you.

LANG What will I have?

HOMER You'll have what you've always had.

You'll have your things.

LANG My . . . ?

HOMER Your collection.

Your duffel.

LANG *(looks around, distant)* Yes . . .

But Homer?

HOMER Yes, Lang?

LANG What's the use of duffel . . . without love?

HOMER *turns in* LANG*'s direction. Gradually, he smiles. Then he goes very still.*

LANG *(after a moment)* Homer . . . ?

(He draws closer.)

Homer . . . ?

Closer still. LANG *stares at* HOMER, *then shuts his brother's eyes with two fingers. A moment.*

N-O-O-O-O-O-O-O-O-O-O-O!

He charges a hill of junk, throws himself on it, slides down. Then he rushes to the pulley system that runs the junk trap, reaches for it, can't bring himself to do it. He just stands for a moment, lost. Then, like a mantra:

Everything that is, is fine; everything that is, is fine; everything that is, is . . .

He lifts his head to look at HOMER. *Stiltedly, he rises and crosses to him. Circles his body. Then he props* HOMER *up in the chair, arranges him until he takes on the aspect of a statue. He walks back to a chair.*

All right . . . all right . . . all right . . . all right . . .

(LANG *seats himself across from* HOMER.)

Just don't move . . .

(LANG *tilts his head and contemplates his brother.*)

Just—please!—don't move . . .

FADE OUT.

EVERETT
BEEKIN

EVERETT BEEKIN was produced in November 2001 in New York City by the Lincoln Center Theater, André Bishop, artistic director; Bernard Gersten, executive producer. It was directed by Evan Yionoulis; set design was by Christopher Barreca; lighting design was by Donald Holder; costume design was by Teresa Snider-Stein; and original music and sound design was by Mike Yionoulis. The stage manager was Denise Yaney. The casting was by Daniel Swee.

The cast was as follows:

MA/WAITRESS
Marcia Jean Kurtz

SOPHIE/CELIA
Robin Bartlett

ANNA/NELL
Bebe Neuwirth

JACK/BEE
Jeff Allin

MIRI/LAUREL
Jennifer Carpenter

JIMMY/EV
Kevin Isola

The play was commissioned and first produced by the South Coast Repertory in September 2000.

PART ONE

"THE SHABBOS GOY"

SETTING

A tenement apartment on the Lower East Side of Manhattan. Summer, 1947.

CHARACTERS

MA—sixties

SOPHIE—late thirties

JACK—late thirties

ANNA—a couple of years younger than Sophie

JIMMY—twenties

MIRI—twenties

ANNA, SOPHIE, JACK, *and* MA.

Plenty of food.

JACK *eating a vast deli sandwich.*

MA *Shah!*

SOPHIE I wasn't talking loudly; was I talking loudly?

JACK Good brisket.

SOPHIE Don't eat with your mouth full.

MA Your sister.

ANNA *(filing her nails)* Summer colds are the worst.

SOPHIE Remember how many I used to get?

ANNA Who wants to be sick when it's hot?

SOPHIE Remember?

ANNA No.

SOPHIE Sure. In the summers. Ma, do you remember?

MA *Wuss?*

ANNA Ma, don't say "*wuss.*" Say "what."

MA I want you should talk more quietly.

ANNA From the womb to Delancey Street, so why is she
    talking like this?

MA Miri needs her sleep.

JACK These pickles are good.

ANNA So how's your truck, Jack?

JACK Good, thank you, very good.

ANNA Are you enjoying it?

JACK It's very good.

ANNA As long as you enjoy it.

SOPHIE Does Abe enjoy his work?

ANNA No.

SOPHIE You do what you do. Are you still going to the library
    so much?

ANNA Half a dozen books, I've read them all. I go back, I read
   them again.

SOPHIE You should *buy* a book from time to time.

ANNA Buy a *book*?

SOPHIE If you're so dissatisfied with the library.

ANNA Who said I'm dissatisfied?

SOPHIE You said they don't have anything.

ANNA You're reading in.

MA So, Jack, you got for me a *bissel* something?

JACK *(handing her a roll of bills from his shirt pocket)*
   Here you go, Gussie.

MA Thanks.

JACK Don't mention it.

MA *(looking at ANNA)* Mm?

ANNA How much did Sophie give, Ma?

SOPHIE Fifteen; you know what I give.

ANNA *(forks over a single bill)* Here, Ma, take twenty. From
   me and Abe both.

MA Very good.

SOPHIE He must be doing nicely.

ANNA There's the house, but knock wood.

SOPHIE So is he a real actuary yet?

ANNA What does that mean, is he a real actuary? Of course
   he's a real actuary.

SOPHIE Is he certified?

ANNA No.

SOPHIE What, he's afraid of the tests?

ANNA He's not afraid of them, he doesn't want to take
   them.

SOPHIE What kind of craziness is that?

ANNA He says he doesn't want to be hemmed in.

SOPHIE Agh, that's craziness. Speaking of which, how is his nervous breakdown going?

ANNA Abe is not, *was* not, having a nervous breakdown.

SOPHIE Call it what you will.

ANNA He got a little tense.

SOPHIE He couldn't sleep, he couldn't *eat*! And with that stomach on him.

ANNA He's flat as a board.

SOPHIE Believe me, it's coming. So what was it if not a breakdown?

ANNA It happens to newlywed men often.

SOPHIE Who told you that?

ANNA An expert.

SOPHIE In what field?

ANNA Sophie—

SOPHIE What sort of expert told you that it wasn't a nervous breakdown?

ANNA If you must know, a psychologist.

SOPHIE Ah-*hah*!

ANNA What is that finger in the air, it's a meaningless gesture to me.

SOPHIE All I know is it didn't happen to Jack when we got married.

ANNA Jack is not exactly what you would call a complicated person. How's the brisket, Jack, are you enjoying?

JACK *(mouthful)* Very good, very good.

SOPHIE You think the brisket is good?

JACK Very good.

SOPHIE What are you, crazy? You could make shoes from it. No offense, Ma. Her brisket has always been terrible, don't you think she makes a terrible brisket?

ANNA I'm not a brisket fan. Ma, please don't do that.

MA *has been dunking the bills into a tub of suds and hanging them from an indoor clothesline.*

MA *Wuss?*

ANNA I beg you.

MA This way it dries.

ANNA I beg you.

MA This way it's clean.

ANNA The neighbors.

SOPHIE It's a *shanda*.

MA The neighbors can't see.

SOPHIE The neighbors can't see, why are you so concerned. Ma, has Leah given with an open hand or no?

MA Money?

SOPHIE Yes.

MA My sister, may she one day rest in peace, gives *bubkus*.

ANNA Oh, that's a pity.

SOPHIE That's a shame. You can console yourself, Ma, you've got at least two less chins. Don't you think Leah has the head of an elephant?

ANNA *Shah*.

SOPHIE I'm not saying to be rude, I'm being factual.

ANNA Sometimes it's the same thing.

SOPHIE I always thought she had the head of an elephant. Even when she was skinny.

ANNA Leah was never skinny.

SOPHIE Compared to what she is now, she was skinny.

ANNA Compared to what she is *now*, I-don't-*know*-what is skinny.

SOPHIE Abe in ten years.

ANNA Abe plays ball.

SOPHIE Mark my words.

JACK Miri looks very thin.

ANNA "Feed a cold, starve a fever."

SOPHIE What are you talking about, Jack? You don't know what you're talking about.

JACK Very thin.

SOPHIE You think this is a good brisket, your opinion is of no importance.

JACK A thin girl.

SOPHIE Should we be making her eat? "Feed a cold, starve—"

ANNA No, no, that means *if* you feed a cold, you will *later* starve a fever.

SOPHIE That's not what that means.

ANNA Yes, yes, that's what that means.

SOPHIE What do you do, sit in your Levitt house and make these things up?

ANNA It happens to be true.

SOPHIE Maybe the next town has a better library, something to *while* away your time. "*If* you feed a cold, you will *later*—" Whoever heard of such thing?

ANNA When are you moving?

SOPHIE We're thinking of it.

ANNA They're building all over the island. Abe and I could show you around.

SOPHIE We're thinking Westchester.

ANNA Westchester?

SOPHIE Yes.

ANNA Westchester *County*?

SOPHIE Yes.

ANNA *(sniffs)* . . . Well. If you want to live with people from the Bronx.

SOPHIE What's wrong with people from the Bronx? The Grand Concourse has some very nice types, Riverdale.

ANNA Those people don't move to Westchester. They don't have an incentive. It's people from I-don't-*know*-where the Bronx.

SOPHIE You're a spinner of tales.

ANNA At any rate, it's not urgent.

SOPHIE Meaning?

ANNA You're not crowded for space.

SOPHIE How are you going to fit the baby in that house?

ANNA There's a room for the baby.

SOPHIE *Room*, yes; *space*, no. What are you naming it?

ANNA If it's a boy, Stephen.

SOPHIE That name's very popular now.

ANNA And for a girl, Celia.

SOPHIE Also Bruce. Everywhere you go, Bruce *Drucker*, Bruce *Fineman*, Bruce *Plotkin*—*Celia?* Off of what rooftop did that fly from?

ANNA Did you see *Brief Encounter*?

SOPHIE You're going to name her after that plain actress?

ANNA I like the name!

SOPHIE If you want your daughter to be a plain English actress, it's perfect.

ANNA I like the sound.

SOPHIE Whatever. God willing, it won't be a girl.

ANNA I'd like a girl.

SOPHIE Just don't name a boy Pete.

ANNA Who's naming a boy Pete so fast?

SOPHIE It's the name of a *handyman*.

ANNA Are you still thinking of adopting?

(Beat.)

MA *Wuss?*

ANNA Ma, say "what."

SOPHIE Don't talk in front of Ma.

MA Adopting?

SOPHIE Nobody has spoken here.

MA You mustn't.

SOPHIE Ma, your money, it must be time to rinse.

MA What if you get a *shaigetz*?

ANNA Ma!

SOPHIE What are you, crazy?

ANNA They don't do interfaith, Ma.

MA They could switch on you.

ANNA They don't do that, Ma.

MA The Jews these days: very popular.

SOPHIE Oh yes, I've noticed.

MA Every home wants one, like you should be an ap*pli*ance.

SOPHIE My coming-out at the Waldorf was such a thing!
   Brenda Diana Duff Frazier was green!

MA I'm talking the *emmis*.
      They could switch on you.
      They could give you a gentile.

SOPHIE Ma? Anna knows this very nice psychologist you might
   want to talk to. About his credentials, I can't testify—
   evidently, he doesn't know a nervous breakdown when he
   sees one—but maybe you'd be better off anyway.
      (to ANNA*)* Are you listening to your mother? Do you
   believe?

ANNA *Shah.*

SOPHIE Why *"shah"*? You're the one who's saying.

MA They give you a little one—what do you know from it?
   They all come out the same hole. A few days pass, Jew, not

Jew, it's a boy, they whack it off. *(illustrates with a swipe of the brisket knife, which passes under* JACK's *nose)* Then, one day, in the development of time, you see it doesn't got a nose on its face to call its own. By then, too late.

SOPHIE We think we might want a child.

MA So, *nu? Have* a child.

SOPHIE All right, Ma, that's what we'll do.

MA Or don't. What, they keep you out of Westchester you don't have little ones?

SOPHIE It seems that way, Ma.

MA There's a guard at the border?

SOPHIE It seems that way.

MA *Pah!*

SOPHIE Whatever, Ma, whatever.

MA Get a *house*.

SOPHIE We'd like to do that, Ma.

MA Keep a room for me.

SOPHIE Sure, Ma.

MA You can be like a lady of leisure, like. I'll cook.

SOPHIE Don't spoil your chances.

MA I always liked the country. Your *father*, may he rot in hell (may he rest in peace), you couldn't scratch out of bed to look at a tree. He didn't know from a flower. So he dies. A fat lot of good it does him, his *city*. His "tall buildings." Listen, I want you should know, if I drop dead tonight on the sidewalk of a heart condition, don't ever let a kind word pass your lips to my sister.

ANNA We won't, Ma.

SOPHIE Maybe people aren't drinking these days.

MA My *bubeleh*, you're an idiot.

ANNA The Irish alone, in that neighborhood—

MA She's a rich woman. With plenty of money, which she never tires of not giving me any. Furs. Just yesterday, didn't Mrs. Abrams see her in the street with her mink down to the floor?

SOPHIE In July.

ANNA She must have been *shvitz*ing.

SOPHIE She was wearing her fur yesterday?

ANNA She's the size of I don't-*know*-what.

MA And the *younger* sister. With a husband alive the way he is. And a *tee*totaler in spite he owns a liquor store.

ANNA This is true; Manny doesn't drink.

SOPHIE Who worked at the store, you or me?

ANNA Does he drink?

SOPHIE No. Manny doesn't drink.

ANNA So, why are you contradicting?

JACK I'm going for a smoke.

ANNA Do you have mentholated?

JACK What are you talking?

ANNA Never mind.

SOPHIE Since when do you smoke mentholated?

ANNA With the baby, I figured . . .

SOPHIE The baby doesn't like the taste?

JACK I'm gonna have a little walk.

He exits.

MA And Barney's no better.

ANNA He's sweet, Uncle Barney.

SOPHIE Barney gives with an open fist. Barney gives you money, Ma.

MA He makes me a beggar in the street.

ANNA He bought us schoolbooks.

MA My daughters, let me advise you one thing: don't be related
to nobody.

MIRI *(offstage)* Ma?

MA Coming, darling, coming. I don't want you should strain.
(Pause.)

SOPHIE Why are you like this?

ANNA How am I?

SOPHIE Don't pretend with me. You know how you are.

ANNA Sophie, you're confusing me.

SOPHIE Don't be like yourself.

Pause. SOPHIE *gets up, crosses the room, and looks out the
window.*

ANNA So who should I be like?

SOPHIE *(clipped)* I don't. Care. To discuss it.
(Pause.)

ANNA Do you want to talk about something else?

SOPHIE I don't mind.
  I'm amenable.
(Pause.)

ANNA Why Westchester?

SOPHIE What, it's got to be follow the leader?
  You're the *younger* sister.
(Beat.)

ANNA Miri's younger still.

SOPHIE Summer colds. Do you remember how many of them I
used to get?

ANNA No.

SOPHIE You don't remember anything. Where were you during the days of our growing up, Buckingham Palace?

ANNA I was bookish.

(Beat.)

They don't switch like Ma said. She's gone nutty.

SOPHIE There are difficulties.

ANNA I'd figured.

SOPHIE Agh.

In a way I'm grateful.

I don't have to be dutiful on Saturday nights anymore.

MA *reenters.*

MA My Miri needs water.

ANNA Is she coming out? We haven't even said hello.

MA A *bissel* later. *(scurries back in with water)*

SOPHIE When we had colds, did we ask for anything?

ANNA We were never the baby.

SOPHIE If we had a cold, it was "For this you don't miss school." *Malaria*, she'd say, "Buy me a pop from the ice-cream man."

ANNA She's more delicate.

SOPHIE *(skeptical noise)* Hmmph.

ANNA And what is that?

SOPHIE So you're a believer in this cold?

ANNA She has a light summer—

SOPHIE How often do we come here?

ANNA . . . What are you—?

SOPHIE Answer my question: How many times?

ANNA Once a week.

SOPHIE And how many once-a-weeks do we see Miri?

ANNA We see Miri when we see Miri.

SOPHIE My point!

ANNA . . . What point? You have no point.

SOPHIE Her we see once every two months, maybe. Five
    minutes for saying good-bye.

ANNA That's—

SOPHIE She's out with *friends*, so sorry she couldn't get out of
    it—she's having to *work* all of a sudden of a weekend day.
    Believe me, there's no cold. Maybe *sniffles*. And she thinks:
    Ah-hah! This week's excuse!

ANNA What are you talking?

SOPHIE She doesn't want to see us. She fears seeing us.

ANNA Have your head examined.
    What is she afraid of?

SOPHIE Contamination.

ANNA Oy.

SOPHIE She thinks compared to us, she's a different idea. She's
    afraid we're *catching*.

ANNA She's not afraid of us.
    . . . Maybe of *you*.

SOPHIE Meaning?

ANNA Meaning nothing. Don't ask me "meaning." I'm not
    meaning, I'm *talking*.

SOPHIE I know whereof I speak.
    Even the *thinness*.

ANNA She's small-boned.

SOPHIE She's com*pet*itively small-boned.

ANNA Are you drinking Manny's liquor?

SOPHIE We all go up and down—except she's never up. And
    when we go down, she goes more down. When we're sticks,
    she's a twig. If we're twigs, she's a *needle*—

ANNA Sophie—

SOPHIE You've never noticed this?

ANNA You're a crazy person.

SOPHIE She's a "singer." She looks like Merle Oberon.

Do people say these sentences about us?

ANNA They don't apply.

SOPHIE One day she'll be standing in the hole of a piano,
singing "Stormy Weather." Hollywood will call—followed by
the pope to kiss her ring—this is the scenario of her life.

ANNA And what if it is?

SOPHIE I'm not saying, I'm just saying.

(Beat.)

The two of us . . . formerly her sisters.

(Beat.)

She has a cold like I have a fortune of money.

(Beat.)

She's ashamed; so be it.

ANNA She's so much younger. A different generation almost.

(Beat.)

SOPHIE Why, do you think, was she born?

ANNA *Shah!*

SOPHIE I'm not asking mean. I'm asking *casual.*

What's your opinion of her birth?

(Beat.)

ANNA So she was an accident. Case closed.

SOPHIE *(intense whisper)* How could they have an accident?

How could they have an accident?

What was the thinking behind it?

ANNA These things happen.

SOPHIE So . . . you mean . . . they were volun*teers*?

ANNA We don't know what goes on behind closed doors.

SOPHIE *(intense whisper)* When were the doors ever closed?
I defy you to remember a closed door in this house.

Who knew from private?

ANNA So we were away sometimes.

SOPHIE I was always here—till the day of my wedding, I was
in this room.

ANNA You exaggerate.

SOPHIE Or why else would I be married?

ANNA You fell in love.

SOPHIE With *Jack*?

Please, between sisters, no bitter jokes.

But this is another story entirely. I'm just trying to know
the hows and whens.

ANNA There was camp that time; you worked in Manny's liquor
store.

SOPHIE That was later.

ANNA Camp wasn't.

SOPHIE All the crazy socialists. With their books.

ANNA They gave us fresh air, you can't disagree with that.

SOPHIE They were the palest people I ever saw, with their
"fresh air."

They all stayed in their cabins. "Reading."

So that's when they made Miri.

(Beat. They think.)

ANNA Must have been.

Or when they sent us to the corner for bread.

SOPHIE Pop was a slow-moving man.

ANNA That's true.

SOPHIE From the table to the sink, you could gather a minyan.

ANNA When we went to camp, then.

Maybe that's why we went.

SOPHIE You think they had such smarts?

ANNA You never know.

SOPHIE You think . . . they *liked* it?

ANNA I don't speculate.

SOPHIE *(sighs)* People's wants.

MA *comes bustling out of the room, closing the door behind her, heading toward the window.*

MA *Schvindler . . . gonniff . . .*

ANNA Ma, what?

MA He's coming . . .

ANNA Who? Who's coming?

MA Like a hoot owl you sound. "Who-who"—him! The lover-
   boy—

SOPHIE Do you know what she's talking about?

MA The giver of colds.
   (leaning out the window, in a loud whisper) Hey, you!
   I know what you're thinking, and don't get up your hopes.
   Up here you're not a welcome person.

JIMMY *(offstage)* Mrs. Fox—

MA What, you think she wants to see you, you're so
   handsome? Another time, when we're all dead and buried
   and forgotten.

JIMMY I'll be up in a second.

MA You don't got ears in your face to tell the brain in your
   head—which you also don't got—stay away, sonny-boy?
   Already he's on the way.

ANNA Is this Miri's fella?

SOPHIE Miri's got a fella?

ANNA Didn't you know?

SOPHIE No.

ANNA That's funny.

MA Go. Stand in front of the door. Push.

ANNA Ma, don't be ridiculous.

MA Help me push.

SOPHIE So what's his name?

ANNA What is it? Jimmy, Ma?

MA Push—push—

SOPHIE Uh-huh. I see. Jimmy what?

ANNA What's Jimmy's last name, Ma?

MA Push—pu—

ANNA Nobody's gonna push, so stop already. When she *gets* like this.

MA *(defeated, moves from the door)* Why? Why do I have a life?

ANNA What's his last name?

MA It's Constant.

ANNA It's not so constant, you have plenty of nice times. You've got the movies, you've got cards with the ladies.

MA It's his name!

ANNA What is?

    Constant?

    (She bursts out laughing.)

    Oh! I thought—oh—ha-ha-ha-ha!

SOPHIE What kind of name is that, Constant?

ANNA *Goyishe.*

SOPHIE I know that, but even so.

ANNA So, is he a nice boy?

SOPHIE "Johnson" is a name. "Smith" is a name. "Constant" is a word.

MA He's a *thief.*

JIMMY *enters.*

JIMMY Hello.
>   *(He sees the hanging money.)*
>   I see you've hung pennants for the Fourth.

He laughs, it peters out.
Beat.

SOPHIE So you must be this Jimmy.
JIMMY I am, yes.
MA Listen here, boychick—
JIMMY Mrs. Fox, Miri asked me.
MA By the stroke of five, I want you should be gone.
JIMMY It's already after six.
MA *(holding up the flat of her hand)*—fingers against your
>   fresh cheek, sonny-boy.
ANNA *(extends her hand)* I'm Anna, Miri's older sister, and
>   this is Sophie, Miri's even older sister.
JIMMY How are you? So good to meet you. She did ask me to
>   come, I'm not improvising that.
ANNA Of course. I'm sure she did.
>   She's unfortunately down with a cold.
SOPHIE "Down with a cold"?
ANNA But perhaps when she awakens—
JIMMY Oh, she's asleep?
SOPHIE Yes, but "perhaps when she awakens," you may see
>   her, mayhaps.
MIRI *(offstage)* Ma . . .
JIMMY Oh!

MA I'm coming— *(to* JIMMY*)* You, no.
    Eat and go.

She exits.
The three are alone.

JIMMY Hi.

ANNA *(pleasantly indicating he should sit)* Please. So, how
    did you meet Miriam?

JIMMY Oh! At a victory canteen.

ANNA I worked at those from time to time.

JIMMY Oh, really?

ANNA We live on the island now.

JIMMY It's nice there.

ANNA In Levittown for the time being, but later on, you never
    know.

JIMMY Is that nice there?

ANNA Quite pleasant, quite pleasant. Not pa*l*atial, but
    everyone's young. Good for the babies.

JIMMY How many children do you have?

ANNA I'm expecting my first.

JIMMY Oh. Congratulations.

ANNA Two years after, I'll have my next.

JIMMY You have it planned.

ANNA I feel I can afford to. There are no problems for me in
    that regard, knock wood.

JIMMY I bet Levittown's a great place for children.

SOPHIE They were going to call it Island Trees.

JIMMY Is that right?

ANNA Yes, in fact.

SOPHIE Then they looked around, no trees.

ANNA They planted them subsequently.

SOPHIE It was embarrassing; they had to change the name.

ANNA They're growing very fast.

SOPHIE And what was your name before they changed it, Mr. Constant?

JIMMY It's always been Constant.

ANNA That's a funny remark.

SOPHIE We have been Fox ever since my grandfather took over Fox's deli and couldn't afford to change the sign.

ANNA Why don't you eat something, Sophie?

SOPHIE So you met at the victory canteen?

JIMMY Yes. Uh-huh.

SOPHIE Uh-huh.

     So then you don't work in Miri's place of business?

JIMMY Oh no, not at all.

SOPHIE She's a secretary, you know. For lawyers.

ANNA I was a secretary, too. An executive secretary. I've retired. I don't have the need of work.

SOPHIE Then you're not necessarily a lawyer.

JIMMY No.

     I'm not a lawyer.

SOPHIE Uh-huh. I see.

     So you met at the canteen?

JIMMY Yes.

SOPHIE So you were in the war?

JIMMY No. Just the army.

     I didn't go overseas.

SOPHIE Uh-huh. I see.

     So were you in school or working at some career or—

ANNA What do you do for a living, for God's sake?

JIMMY Business.

I'm a businessman.

(Pause.)

SOPHIE Okay.

(Pause.)

JIMMY Well, I'm going to be a businessman.

(Pause.)

SOPHIE Uh-huh. I see.

JIMMY I *was* in school. College.

ANNA Where was that?

JIMMY Bucknell. In Pennsylvania.

ANNA O-h-h-h-h-h: foliage.

JIMMY And then I went into the army. But the war was almost over.

SOPHIE I didn't go to college.

ANNA I didn't, either.

SOPHIE We were poor as dirt.

ANNA Not *dirt*.

SOPHIE Dirt.

ANNA I had to forgo a Regent's scholarship.

SOPHIE I worked in a liquor store.

ANNA Miri and I took a secretarial course in high school.

SOPHIE I miss selling.

ANNA But I'm Pitman, she's Gregg—different worlds, you know.

SOPHIE *(to* JIMMY*)* That's shorthand. *(to* ANNA*)* He doesn't know Gregg and Pitman, why are you talking that way?

Her husband, who is in the office today working his way into an early grave, sometimes says "chahk-let." For candy.

JIMMY Is that right?

ANNA No.

SOPHIE I'm just saying!

JIMMY Do you think Miri will be coming out soon?

ANNA It's hard to say. She's exhausted, poor thing.

SOPHIE She has a light summer cold. According to legend.

JIMMY On the phone, she sounded—

SOPHIE You spoke on the phone?

JIMMY She called me from a drugstore yesterday; she
    sounded—

ANNA She called you from a drugstore?

JIMMY Yes. She sounded—

SOPHIE Where do you live?

JIMMY Brooklyn. Brooklyn Heights.

SOPHIE From the drugstore she got Brooklyn Heights?

JIMMY No. She called me at work. She sounded—

ANNA What is your place of employment?

JIMMY I work, for the time being, in a small accounting firm.
    Midtown.

ANNA Oh, from the drugstore you can call there; it's all right.

JIMMY She told me to come over today. She sounded—

SOPHIE So you're an accountant?

JIMMY No. That's just temporary—

ANNA Because you don't seem the accountant type.

JIMMY What's the accountant type?

ANNA There's a certain type.

JIMMY I—

SOPHIE Saul Weintraub from the neighborhood became an
    accountant—

ANNA Nobody lifted an eyebrow—

SOPHIE He was the type—

ANNA For his whole life, you knew—

SOPHIE In the crib, it was evident what would become of
    him—

ANNA You wouldn't fit with him.

SOPHIE Could you imagine them at lunchtime?

ANNA No.

SOPHIE They'd go their separate ways.

ANNA Saul would remain at his desk with an egg.

SOPHIE You I could see at Luchow's. You and Saul have no
    future together.

JIMMY I'm . . . sorry to hear that. *(He laughs politely.)*

ANNA His loss.

    (Pause.)

    So.

    You met at the victory canteen.

JIMMY Uh, yes.

SOPHIE Who picked up who?

ANNA *Shah!*

SOPHIE Of *Iran.*

ANNA Don't talk like that—

SOPHIE If you don't stop with the *shah*ing me, I don't *know*
    what—and I *mean* that.

JIMMY It wasn't like that. We . . . started talking. It was . . . like
    that.

ANNA You mingled.

JIMMY We struck up a conversation.

ANNA You were friendly.

JIMMY She said I could come home with her and be the
    shabbos goy—that's a gentile who comes into a Jewish
    home on the Sabbath and does all the things the Jews can't
    do, like turn on electricity and— But you probably already
    know what that is.

SOPHIE Of course.

ANNA A thing there's no need of in this house.

JIMMY I think it was a joke.

SOPHIE "*Shabbos* goy"!

ANNA We touch electricity whenever we please, thank you very much—

SOPHIE What kind of joke is that? The girl is a *mocker*: she *mocks*.

ANNA Friday, Saturday, whenever it strikes our fancy— "I think I'd like a little electricity"— Poof! On it goes!

SOPHIE We're not *shomer shabbos* here—

JIMMY *Shomer sha*—?

ANNA I don't know the meaning of the word anymore.

JIMMY Oh—I thought you didn't eat shrimp here and things like that.

ANNA We don't eat shrimp here because nobody has a recipe.

SOPHIE It's not, you should excuse the expression, for "religious reasons."

ANNA We live modern.

SOPHIE Mod-dren, that's us.

JIMMY Oh.

SOPHIE Go to a shtetl if you don't want shrimp.

JIMMY I like shrimp.

SOPHIE Good. Maybe you'll take us to Luchow's sometime.

ANNA To the '21' club.

JIMMY Maybe so, yes.

SOPHIE Not eat shrimp; what has Miri been telling you, stuffing your head with lies?

ANNA Miriam is not a liar.

SOPHIE Her whole life.

ANNA She's good as gold.

SOPHIE From the time she was this high—

ANNA Those weren't lies, that was *play*. She was a child. She
embellished.

SOPHIE Oh, I see. Very good.

Jimmy, did you know that my husband, smoking on the
stoop at present, owns the biggest fleet of large commercial
trucks in America?

I'm em*bel*lishing.

ANNA Why are you in this mood?

JIMMY When is your child due?

ANNA Five months.

JIMMY Have you picked out a name?

ANNA Stephen, if it's a boy—

SOPHIE Anything but Pete.

ANNA —and for a girl, Celia.

JIMMY Celia!

That's a very nice name.

SOPHIE After the actress in *Brief Encounter.*

JIMMY She's an excellent actress.

Quite plain.

SOPHIE HAH!

JIMMY And do you have children?

SOPHIE . . . We're looking.

JIMMY I think it's very wise of you to live out of the city. If
you're going to have children.

ANNA Oh yes. The city is fine in youth, but once you've taken
on adult responsibilities—

SOPHIE It's like Princess Elizabeth stopped in for a nice glass
tea—

ANNA Room and fresh air are essential.

SOPHIE Get her.

JIMMY I'm going to be moving soon myself.

ANNA And where would that be to?

JIMMY California.

(Beat.)

SOPHIE O-h-h-h-h-h.

JIMMY Southern California.

ANNA Los Angeles?

JIMMY South of that a little.

ANNA A-a-a-a-a-h-h.

SOPHIE So then you won't be seeing Miri much?

JIMMY I hope I *will*.

(Beat. The sisters move in closer.)

ANNA So what is it you'll be doing out there?

SOPHIE Have you got a plan, or are you thinking gold mines
and eureka?

JIMMY There's this fellow I met in the army I'm going to be
starting up a business with. Pharmaceuticals.

ANNA You're gonna be a druggist.

JIMMY Not exactly. He's a chemical genius. He's going to
research and develop drugs and manufacture them—

ANNA He needs California for that?

JIMMY It's this wonderful area— They call it Orange County.

ANNA Orange County!

JIMMY It's so beautiful—there's almost nothing there—

SOPHIE Covered wagons.

ANNA Hush.
      Why California?

JIMMY What's wrong with California?

SOPHIE It's not home.

(Beat.)

JIMMY It will be.

SOPHIE For some, yes; for others, don't get your hopes up.

. . . And what is this fella's name, the druggist?

JIMMY Everett Beekin—

SOPHIE Hoo-*hoo*—

JIMMY —the Sixth.

SOPHIE The *Sixth*?

JIMMY Yes.

ANNA That's too many.

JIMMY Well, actually—

SOPHIE Why does one family need so many Everett Beekins?
It's nutty.

JIMMY Actually, there's a funny story behind that. Would you
like to hear it?

(Beat. The sisters look at each other.)

ANNA Not really.

SOPHIE No, I don't think so.

ANNA We're not one for stories, really.

JIMMY Oh.

. . .

. . .

Listen, are you sure she really has a cold?

On the phone, it sounded like—

ANNA This is Miri.

SOPHIE She's *frail*. When necessary.

ANNA She's the baby.

SOPHIE She's the baby, she got pampered.

ANNA So things, when they happen to her, are bigger than for
other people.

SOPHIE For a cold, think a normal person's pneumonia.

ANNA It's just a cold, but she acts like—

SOPHIE She acts like it's I-don't-*know*-what.

ANNA Pop died soon after she was born.

SOPHIE Minutes.

ANNA Not *minutes*—

SOPHIE It was foolish even leaving the hospital—

ANNA So Ma felt that with the nice parent gone, she had to do an imitation.

SOPHIE That's true.

ANNA Not for us. Just for Miri.

SOPHIE That's true.

ANNA In consequence, Miri's always been susceptible. You should know this. For future reference.

SOPHIE Which you won't need, because your idea of the *suburbs* is California. Ta-ta to you.

JIMMY I don't think that's true.

(Beat.)

SOPHIE Have you made promises to each other?

(Beat.)

JIMMY Are you on my side?

SOPHIE On your side? I don't *know* you! You walked in off the street. For all I know, you're here to sell ice.

ANNA Of course we're on your side.

Why not?

SOPHIE A better question: Why?

ANNA I like his looks.

SOPHIE *(a contemptuous noise)*

ANNA I don't mean he's nice-*looking*; I mean he looks nice.

SOPHIE Tell me, uh, Jimmy: this Everett Beeson—

JIMMY Beekin.

SOPHIE *Now* it's Beekin.

How would you describe *his* looks?

JIMMY Uh, well— He's several years older—

SOPHIE Uh-huh. I see. Than *you*?

JIMMY Yes. He's in his early forties. He wasn't even drafted: he signed up.

SOPHIE But other than that, he resembles . . . ?

JIMMY Well . . .

I guess . . .

Sort of *me*, actually.

SOPHIE Ah-hah!

JIMMY Ah-hah?

ANNA I don't get what I just learned.

SOPHIE It's like with the *schvartzes*.

ANNA Not schvartzes, *col*ored. Besides, you mean the Chinese.

JIMMY I'm—lost?—

SOPHIE Either way, you want little nephews, little nieces, that look like him?

ANNA Yes.

(Pause.)

SOPHIE I wash my hands of this part of you.

ANNA What would be so bad?

Who's the prettiest one in the room at the moment?

SOPHIE I wash my hands—

ANNA Why shouldn't people look like that?

I wouldn't mind if Stephen or Celia looked like this boy.

SOPHIE I wish you luck. Married to your Abe with the nose like a Watusi.

ANNA Anyway, when did this get to be the point?

JIMMY Have I done something wrong?

SOPHIE Almost certainly.

ANNA Tell me, Jimmy: Have you proposed?

(Pause.)

JIMMY Yes.

(Beat.)

SOPHIE Uh-huh. I see.

ANNA And has she given you any indication?

JIMMY She's accepted.

(Beat.)

SOPHIE *(to* ANNA*)* And you say she's not a liar.

ANNA I'm sure she's sincere.

SOPHIE But did she say to us word one—?

ANNA She keeps secrets—

SOPHIE She's a secret-keeper—

ANNA That's not the same as a liar. Everybody keeps secrets. I
keep secrets.

SOPHIE Only your own. Mine you broadcast to the four
winds—

ANNA Hush!

SOPHIE And don't think I don't know that "hush" is just "shah"
with the letters shuffled.

ANNA *(to* JIMMY*)* So she told you yes?

JIMMY Yes.

ANNA That's romantic.

JIMMY We should lower our voices. Your mother doesn't know
yet, and she doesn't like me.

ANNA Don't say "doesn't like."

SOPHIE Say "hate." She *hates* you.

ANNA You don't know.

SOPHIE Oh, please.

JIMMY It's true. I come here, I feel like Rapunzel.

ANNA Uh-huh.

JIMMY I mean, like the prince.

SOPHIE *Some*one not real.

JIMMY I don't think she really has a cold.

SOPHIE This is what I'm saying.

JIMMY I think she's being kept from me.

SOPHIE . . . This is a new theory.

JIMMY Your mother does that. She's a very powerful woman.

ANNA Ma? No.

SOPHIE Ma's not powerful.

ANNA Ma has no power.

SOPHIE A *nasty* woman, yes, but powerful—

JIMMY She does this. She's done it before.

Miri is very obedient, very suggestible. (SOPHIE *makes a fleering sound.*) No, she is.

When your mother knows I'm coming, she keeps Miri from seeing me. She finds ways.

I want to make your sister happy.

That's all I want.

Since I met her.

I—

I'm going to do very well in the world.

I'm going to thrive.

It's so obvious, I don't feel the need of modesty.

This isn't boasting!

Look at the country now. Look at me.

There won't be a problem.

When I got out of the army . . . It's not that I wasn't looking forward to life. I just wasn't . . . thrilling to the idea.

Do you know?

I was all means and no end.

Then I met Miri.

She's plainly troubled.

ANNA AND SOPHIE *(variously)* What does that mean? . . .

What are you talking? . . . *(et cetera)*

JIMMY But in the most great ways!

She's complicated, her life has been hard—

SOPHIE Puh!

JIMMY Well, it *has*.

SOPHIE Romantic.

ANNA The boy doesn't know from what's hard. It's sweet, let him talk.

SOPHIE *Shah!*

JIMMY I want to make things easy for her.

SOPHIE And what do you have to offer?

JIMMY A future.

SOPHIE At *present*?

(Beat.)

JIMMY A future.

SOPHIE In California with Everett Edward Horton.

JIMMY Beekin.

SOPHIE Pie in the sky.

JIMMY *(suddenly stern)* But it's not.

(lighter)

He's been working at this for fifteen years. For another company—I won't say which.

Some of the drugs we take today—

SOPHIE I don't take drugs—

ANNA Just aspirin—

SOPHIE Not even.

JIMMY —that *people* take were designed by him. Analgesics and tranquilizers, chiefly, for which there's an ever growing market—oh, he's an amazing man! All the Everett Beekins were! They distinguished themselves in so many ways! Doctors and lawyers and ministers and famous writers. My

Mr. Beekin—the Sixth—came out of St. Louis twenty years ago, dirt poor—

SOPHIE Dirt poor?

JIMMY Yes.

ANNA With all those distinguished ancestors, a man should be dirt poor?

JIMMY Well—you see—that was the story— They all vanished—

SOPHIE Huh?

JIMMY The ancestors—somehow everybody's lost track of them— They were distinguished and later invisible.

SOPHIE What kind of *ferkakta* thing is that—

JIMMY I know, this part is fuzzy—

SOPHIE I don't know about these Everett Beekins of yours—

JIMMY I said it was a *story*. I didn't say it made sense—

SOPHIE Puh!

JIMMY But *my* Everett Beekin—Everett Beekin the Sixth—he can be proven.

I mean, he's among us.

ANNA He sounds wonderful!

SOPHIE He sounds like a thief.

JIMMY He just needed someone with a brain for business, and I have that brain.

SOPHIE Feh!

JIMMY You would like him if you knew him. He has this real sweet wife and this really cute little boy.

ANNA What's the little boy's name?

SOPHIE AND JIMMY Everett Beekin the Seventh—

SOPHIE *(to* ANNA*)* Don't you know how this family works yet?

ANNA Oh, of course.

SOPHIE And he's gonna pack the whole bunch of them off to a place where there's nothing and fill it up with drugs.

ANNA I would like that. Maybe someday.

SOPHIE Levittown's such a burden?

JIMMY Your sister will be rich.

ANNA She's difficult.

JIMMY I'll make it easy.

(Beat.)

ANNA I have no objections.

SOPHIE You also have absolutely no say in the matter.

Why would she want to marry this boy?

JIMMY She loves me, she respects me, she's attracted to me, she enjoys my company—

SOPHIE And from this you build a marriage?

ANNA Yes, Sophie.

SOPHIE I don't agree.

JIMMY Your husband has been smoking all this time?

SOPHIE And may it go on forever.

Listen.

You don't marry for those movie reasons.

You marry because life as it is is no longer bearable, so even something else that's terrible looks inviting.

You marry so that one makes money, the other cooks and cleans, at the end of the day, if there's money on the table and a little something to eat on a clean plate, you know the day has made sense.

You marry so that when you get sick of each other's voices, you have a child to add variety, the world continues.

Your reasons, in another year or so, will *embarrass* you.

ANNA I married for love.

SOPHIE And the good it did you? Itemize?

ANNA And now I'm going to have a baby.

SOPHIE Meanwhile, your husband can't join you for a family
meal because he's at his psychiatrist, "working things out."

ANNA Who told you?

SOPHIE What? I'm right? HA!

ANNA *(to* JIMMY*)* Some men—the war—it left them a little
nervous.

SOPHIE What "the war"? It was your wedding made him
nervous. The war he found delightful.

ANNA That's not true.

SOPHIE He was in Hawaii, having luaus—we all should have
had such a war. This husband of hers: a prime candidate for
when your drugs come rolling off the assembly line—

JIMMY I bet they'll work.

ANNA I bet they will.

> *(to* SOPHIE, *defiantly)* I bet they will.

MA *opens the door.*

MA Jimmy—she wants you *out.* She said.

JIMMY I don't believe you.

MA Hah? What are you saying, this *pischer?*

JIMMY I don't believe you, Mrs. Fox. I think you're lying to me.

MA *Wuss?*

JIMMY I think you're keeping her from me.

MA Puh!

JIMMY But it's not going to work. I'm going to marry her.

MA Who is this person?

SOPHIE He makes drugs, and he thinks he's Rapunzel.

JIMMY You have to understand, Mrs. Fox—I *will* make this
happen. I'm not as nice as I look.

MA To me, you look nice like a boil, Jimmy Constantly-gives-
    me-chest-pains.

ANNA Ma, be nice!

JIMMY Come out, Miri!

MA *Shah!* She needs quiet!

JIMMY Miri, please come out!

SOPHIE He's a yeller.

ANNA *Shah!*

JIMMY *Miri!*

MIRI *opens the door. She is ghost white, the color of her
nightgown. She trembles, her hair is wild. She is dying.
The sisters don't acknowledge it.*

JIMMY . . . Miri?

MIRI *(reaches out her hand to him)* Jimmy, could you help
    me?

*He takes her arm and leads her to the one comfortable
chair.*

JIMMY Miri—

SOPHIE Hi, Miri, nice to see you.

MIRI Hi.

ANNA So how are you, sweetie, all stuffed up?

MIRI I have a cold . . . a summer cold.

SOPHIE Summer colds are the worst.

ANNA Oh, yes. Remember how I'd get?

SOPHIE *You?* Me!

JIMMY Miri—?

MIRI I get like this.

JIMMY But—

MIRI It's . . . nothing.

(JIMMY *looks at her and decides it's true.*)

JIMMY Good!

Are you taking anything?

MIRI No . . . it's just a cold.

JIMMY I have some very strong aspirin at home. Not yet on the
market.

MIRI Stay with me a minute.

JIMMY . . . Sure.

*He kneels beside her; she pulls him in to her and strokes
his neck.*

MA You should get back into the bed.

MIRI A minute, Ma—

MA I want you should go to—

MIRI Ma! . . .

MA . . . I'm not talking nothing.

JIMMY Miri—tell your mother, will you? Tell her we're getting
married.

MIRI Yes, Ma, it's true—

MA Mirella—

MIRI It's true, Ma . . . we're getting married.

MA *Shah!*

MIRI Nothing can stop us.

JACK *reenters.*

JACK Howdo, howdo?

SOPHIE Jack, back so soon?

JACK Who's he?

JIMMY *(not leaving* MIRI*)* I'm Jimmy Constant.

JACK Jack Epstein, howdo howdo?

(Silence.)

MIRI I better go back to bed.

She reaches out to JIMMY *for help getting up.*
At the door, she hugs him.

I can make it to the bed.

She disappears into the room.

JIMMY I'm going to get her those aspirin.

I'll be back in a little while. Please don't try to keep me
out.

Really, you can't.

He exits.

JACK That girl is very sick.

SOPHIE What are you with the "very sick"?

ANNA She has a light summer cold.

SOPHIE *(to* JACK*)* Nobody asked your opinion. Ma, we have
to go.

MA *Wuss?*

SOPHIE *(to* ANNA*)* We'll drive you to Penn Station.

ANNA As if you have a choice. Thanks for the delicious supper,
Ma. Same time next week.

MA Next week, yah.

JACK Thankee, thankee, see ya soon, very good.

ANNA Should we say good-bye to Miri?

SOPHIE Nu? She's not sleeping yet. Good-bye, Miri! See you next week!

ANNA Good-bye, Miri! See you next week!

MIRI *(offstage)* . . . Bye.

ANNA Take care of that cold!

SOPHIE See you next week! Come on, Jack, let's go!

JACK Bye-bye, very good, very good.

The three of them are off.
MA *is left alone.*
She looks about the room, looks to the hanging money.
She crosses to MIRI's *room, pauses by it.*
She starts to shake, uncontrollably at first, then forces
herself to stop.

MA *(to nothing)* Shah!

BLACKOUT.

❧ PART TWO ❧

"THE PACIFIC"

SETTING
Orange County, California. The late nineties.

CHARACTERS
NELL—fiftyish
CELIA—a couple of years older
BEE—early fifties
EV—early twenties
LAUREL—early twenties
WAITRESS—sixties

NELL, *on the Unity Bridge.*

NELL Quiet, please, in the back—I'm talking!
     Ahem.
     The Unity Bridge was erected in 1994 and given its name because, in spanning Bristol Street, it unites the forces of Commerce, as represented by the mall, with the Arts, as represented by the bank.
     The life here in Orange County is good and free and new, quite new.
     Historic villages are, I'm afraid, limited to fields of lima beans, and if you wish to meet indigenous peoples, you'd be well advised to loiter on the high school campuses.
     Don't do that, by the way. Security is excellent.
     Eat our food, romp on our beaches, eschew irony, and have a nice day.
     (a touch threatening)
     You *will* here, you know.

Lights.

CELIA, *agitated, in a beachfront house with her trench coat on.*

CELIA And at the hotel! The bell captain or what have you, the person with the tall trolley—when I was checking in, *he* arrived—having just completed some feat of *helpfulness* or other—and the desk clerk, or however he's known, the person taking my credit card—called to him: "Your brother left a message when you were out: he just got back from Tokyo or Japan or someplace like that." Tokyo *or* Japan! Oh! And then the happiness, the greetingness which borders, frankly, on obsession—I mean, the person, the whatever, the *homme de* trolley was with me—I was *trapped* with him on the elevator, and he inquired: "Are you having a great day?" I mean: *great!* The quotidian monumentality of that question boggles the mi— So I said, "Yes, quite satisfactory, thank you. How are you?" And he said: "I'm doing good." And I *winced*, but then I thought, well, no, in a way, yes, after all, people need their valises moved, and you assist in moving them, and that, I suppose, is good, so you are doing *good*, not *well*— I mean, I wanted to rescue *someone's* grammar, because the casualness about that here boggles the mi— And then the smiles, the smiles of menial laborers—the Hertz girl at John Wayne Airport—smiling! Smiles springing up everywhere, like weeds, like fields of purple loosestrife, like artillery fire—I'm not *mixing* metaphors, I'm rolling them over—it makes me want to *duck*! I am so terrified, walking into Vons to buy *Clamato* juice, of being *aggressed* upon by courtesy. I've never experienced anything like it bef— Except once, that one Memorial Day I told you about, that I spent with Jeffrey and his wife and her friends by the Jersey shore—but they were *stewardesses*!

God: those girls! I have never met anyone so *born* to *truckle*. I mean, they were naturally servile. *Nothing* on *earth* made them happier than a request for a refill. It was *appalling*. But the worst part is—and I don't want to mark myself a Californiphobic or someth—because *cliché*—but the worst part is: you can never catch them when you've turned your back and you quick turn back. I mean: the telltale sneer, the exchanged mocking glances. You turn back—and they're still smiling! What *are* they? *Happy?* It gives me the willies! *Is* there to be *no alcohol*?

NELL *(offstage)* I'm still dressing, Celia.

CELIA For Regency England? Are you having trouble with your hoop skirt?

NELL Be *patient*, Celia.

CELIA You started dressing in the late fifties. Aren't you just throwing on slacks?

NELL I'll get you a drink in a mo!

CELIA Don't accessorize. I'd like to get home by 1999.

NELL A martini?

CELIA Very dry; *nothing pink* in it.

NELL Shaken or stirred?

CELIA Stirred. *I'm* shaken.

NELL *enters.*

NELL Just a second.

CELIA God, you look disgustingly spruce.

NELL *(fixing drink)* I'll take that as a compliment.

CELIA Of *course* you will.

NELL I'll ignore that.

CELIA Of *course* you would.

NELL How was the flight?

CELIA The flight?

NELL How was it?

CELIA The flight. Well, the flight was fine. People were surly, babies upchucked, the flight made sense to me; it was lifelike. It was the disembarking when—

NELL *(handing her drink)* —all heaven broke loose.

CELIA Hmph. I suppose that's wit of some kind.

They have handsome homosexual flight attendants now.

NELL And how did you—

CELIA *Won*derfully snide. I love that sort of thing—people of no account judging against you, making their little remarks, catty and impotent, condescending from below. But when you demand the salted peanuts, by God, they have to *get* you the salted peanuts.

NELL Are you seeing anyone?

(Beat.)

CELIA This is an excellent martini.

NELL Laurel should be home in a bit.

CELIA *(vaguely)* Laurel?

NELL Your *niece*, *Cel*ia.

CELIA Well, of course I *know* that.

Oh, that's nice.

Has she become one of those disastrous nihilists her generation puts forth like guppies?

NELL She's quite dear.

They didn't wear hoop skirts in the Regency period.

CELIA Pardon?

NELL It occurred to me.

CELIA Did I say they—?

NELL Yes. Yes, you did. You were wrong.

CELIA Ah.

(Beat.)

Well, I must be unread, then.

I must be simply a pretentious waste of time, then.

My whole life must be some sort of sham.

How good of you, Nell, how *good* and *kind* of you to point this out.

NELL *(Beat.)* How's Mother?

Lights.

CELIA, NELL, *and* BEE *are on the beach:* NELL *in something loose and flowy,* BEE *in shorts and an open shirt,* CELIA *in a long trench coat.*

CELIA Withering.

NELL Hmm?

CELIA Withering away before my very eyes. That terrible translucency their skin takes on.

NELL Who?

CELIA The old.

NELL Oh, the old!

CELIA And she speaks in pure circularities. "When are you leaving?" "Friday." "And why are you going?" "Laurel's wedding." "And where are you staying?" "A hotel." "Oh. When are you leaving?" If only she were an alcoholic or something and there were a pleasant edgelessness to it, but it's all panic.

And testy!

Lies to cover losses, the terrible patchy places—where does it disappear to, the minute before she asks what happened a minute ago? Sad. And fucking tedious.

NELL Who are you talking about, sweetheart?

CELIA Mother.

NELL Oh: Mother. Well, why?

CELIA You asked.

NELL When?

CELIA Before.

NELL Oh, *before*. There's got to be a statute of limitations on
that kind of thing.

CELIA You're as bad as she is.

NELL *rubs suntan lotion on her long bare leg, thrusting it
straight into the sky.*

What's that body of water?

NELL The Pacific.

CELIA Not some . . . inlet . . . or estuary?

NELL No, dear, the whole Pacific.

CELIA *(darkly)* Yes. It would be.

NELL Take off your coat.

CELIA Never.
And she won't leave Hewlett!

NELL Hewlett! Dear Hewlett!

CELIA Oh what is *that*: "Dear Hewlett," as if it's "Greenswards"
or something, the country estate of your drifted youth—it's
Long fucking Island, and it's worse than ever.

NELL Bee, why are you here?

BEE It's a nice place.

CELIA Do you remember when we moved to that house?

NELL No.

CELIA She toured us through the place. "Look, sweeties, all
these rooms! We didn't have *those* in Levittown. Look—
trees! We didn't have *those* in Levittown." As if no one had
ever had rooms. As if there'd never been a tree. "This is our
house!" she said. Then festered there for the next forty—

NELL Bee, are you absolutely sure you're happy here?

BEE You know, I really *am*.

CELIA I worry most about the stairs.

NELL People are going to, if you wear a trench coat on the beach.

CELIA *Flights* of stairs—

NELL Oh—

CELIA For crying out—

NELL So sorry. *(She starts brushing her hair.)*

CELIA She *falls.* Her balance is off. And she's taken to night drives.

NELL You mean drives at night?

CELIA . . . Mm-hm.

NELL Where to?

CELIA Pathmark, Waldbaum's—supermarkets!

NELL Bee, why don't you take a walk?

BEE Lethargic.

CELIA They stay open all night these days. You can imagine the element.

NELL Oh well, it's just the suburbs.

CELIA Long *I*sland! Amy Fisher! Joel Rifkin!

NELL These people are not at Pathmark.

CELIA Their ilk. At that hour. God, the loneliness must be—

BEE I spent some time in Long Island once.

NELL Did you, dear?

BEE Amagansett. There were writers there. Movie people.

CELIA That's a different Long Island.

Something goes whizzing dangerously over their heads; they watch it.

EV *(offstage)* Sorry.

EV *races onstage, wearing trunks and a tank top.*

EV *(on then off)* Sorry sorry sorry—Frisbee. *(And he's gone.)*

CELIA God, your son is good-looking!

BEE My son, yes, he is.

CELIA The brains of lawn furniture, I expect, but—

NELL Celia—!

BEE Isn't he bright? *I* think he is. Does anyone want a
  peach?

NELL AND CELIA *(variously)* No . . . not in the least—

BEE *(stands)* Well, *I* want a peach—

NELL You *are* a peach, dear.

BEE, *smiling, exits.*
A moment.

CELIA The way you flaunt it, it's really—

NELL I am not *flaunting* anything, Celia—oh, how like you to
  be shocked!

CELIA How does this sort of thing tran*spire*, anyway?

NELL Well, we're both practically unmarried—

CELIA And I am *not* shocked, Nell. I am resolutely not—

NELL And our children are getting married—

CELIA How *like* you to think I'd be shocked—

NELL —and we were available to each other—

CELIA *Nothing* is ever a*vail*able.
(Beat.)

NELL Well.

CELIA . . . Is anything going to happen?

NELL Everything has.
  Everything has.

CELIA . . . All I can say is: you are behaving like a much
  younger and prettier woman.

BEE *reenters with three peaches.*

BEE I've brought for everyone.
NELL *(taking one)* Thank you, dear.
*(*BEE *turns to* CELIA, *offers her a peach.)*
CELIA I didn't want one. I said so.
BEE Oh.
EV *(offstage)* Watch out!
BEE *(sees something offstage)* Wow! That nearly clipped that
woman! GOOD SAVE, SON!
EV Thanks.
CELIA What do you do, Bee?
BEE Do?
CELIA For a living?
BEE I no longer have that concern. There were the
pharmaceuticals, of course—
CELIA Pharmaceuticals?
BEE Yes.
CELIA You're *that* Beekin? The pharmaceuticals—
BEE Yes. Well, originally, that was my father—Everett Beekin
the Sixth. I'm Everett Beekin the Seventh. *Ev* is Everett
Beekin the—
CELIA I didn't know you were that Beekin—the
pharmaceuticals—
NELL I'm sure I told you—
CELIA You didn't—
NELL You never listen—
BEE I've mostly retired from all that, anyway. To fill the days
now, I'm a venture capitalist. That means I—
CELIA I had no idea you were that Beekin—
NELL You don't listen—

BEE Does this upset you for some reason? You seem . . . upset
    . . . for some reason.
CELIA . . . No, I . . .
    The flight . . . I'm not an easy traveler.

LAUREL *runs onstage, chasing the Frisbee.*

LAUREL God! I would rather be decapitated by that fucking
    flying disc than have to chase after it one more— *(And
    she's gone.)*
NELL They're very happy together.
CELIA I can't imagine why.
NELL He's a wonderful lover.
    (They look at her).
    My baby and I com*mun*icate.

Lights.

Transition: EV *and* LAUREL *chasing across the stage. They
end up together on the sand.*
NELL *and* CELIA. CELIA *stares straight out.*

NELL Well, that wasn't pure hell for a rehearsal dinner, was it?
    (Beat; no answer.)
    I said: That wasn't pure hell for a rehearsal dinner,
    was it?
    (Again no answer.)
    Celia?
CELIA Oh God, were you talking?

NELL Yes, Celia, I was talking.

CELIA Oh, sorry.

NELL . . .

Are you all right?

Ever since you got here, you've been—

CELIA I'm sorry if I've been in a mood—

NELL You *have*.

CELIA I don't travel well.

NELL I mean, the acid quips I'm used to, but this ab*strac*tion is a new wrinkle in your—

CELIA *(overlaps from "abstraction")* I've been a little spooked lately.

NELL *(continuous)* —arsenal . . . "Spooked"?

CELIA . . . Things keep happening . . . and then *this* place.

NELL What things? What things keep happening?

Tell me.

You should be *able* to tell me.

EV has been tickling LAUREL. CELIA'*s attention is drawn to them.*

LAUREL *(giggling)* Stop it . . . !

EV But—

He continues, while she wriggles free and moves away from him, more seriously.

LAUREL Stop . . .

NELL Celia.

LAUREL Please.

CELIA Nell, there was another sister.

NELL . . .
    Another sister?

    . . .

    We had another—
CELIA Not us. Mother.
NELL Besides Aunt Sophie?
CELIA Yes.
NELL Stillborn?
CELIA Died in her twenties.
NELL Oh, come *on*—
CELIA Deep—rather deep in her twenties—
NELL How do you *know* that?
CELIA Mother.
NELL Mother told you? She *told* you that?
CELIA It came out.
    "Miri," she said one day.
    "When my sister Miri was a girl . . ."
    The way she's been . . . I thought maybe a hallucination . . .
    I asked Aunt Sophie about it just before she died—
NELL You were still talking to Sophie then?
CELIA Yes.
NELL God, she was such a battle-ax! Why would you still be
    talking to—
CELIA She had no children; I filled in.
NELL You're a better man than I am, Gunga—
CELIA She sang.
    (NELL *looks at her.*)
    "Miri."
    She was a singer.
    She looked like Merle Oberon.
    These are the things I was told.

NELL And what did she die of? This "Miri"?

CELIA Some form of cancer that no longer presents a big
    problem. Sophie didn't wish to go into it.

        . . . It seems Miri had a young man. Someone she was
    going to marry. Not Jewish, I gather. They were about to get
    married when she died.

        Miri and . . . this man.

        Sophie said his name was . . . Jimmy Forever.

NELL Jimmy For*ever*?

CELIA Yes.

NELL There can be no such person.

CELIA Sophie's memory wasn't—

NELL That sounds like the name of a *gang*ster in a *mo*vie—

CELIA They'd been planning to get married when she died—
    Sophie said they were planning to get married and move.

        . . . *Here*. Nell, they were going to move *here*—

NELL There was no "here" to speak of then—

CELIA It seems this Jimmy was something of a pioneer. He
    was planning to work with someone—Sophie couldn't
    remember his name—but someone who eventually became
    a tycoon.

        . . . Nell: a pharma*ceu*ticals tycoon.

NELL . . . Oh, you're making this up—

CELIA Sophie said—

NELL Sophie said "pharmaceuticals tycoon"?

CELIA Well, she said "big *macher* druggist," but that's what she
    meant.

        When Bee said—when I realized he was the
    pharma*ceu*ticals Beekin—

NELL There are other people in that field here—

CELIA But *still*.

NELL *makes a little negative sound. She's vaguely disturbed or just pissed off by this whole business and doesn't really hear the rest of* CELIA's *speech.*

Things have been so . . . insisting on themselves lately . . . they've been connecting so strangely . . .

NELL *(having come to a conclusion)* Well—

CELIA I've wanted to *say* something—

NELL Either way—

CELIA I've wanted to say something to someone, but—

NELL Either way, it doesn't really matter, does it? *(Pause.)*

CELIA Doesn't it?

NELL Of course not. If any of this even happened, which I seriously doubt, it was ages ago. Why should it matter?

CELIA Everything seems to, somehow.

NELL . . . That's because you're over*wrought*. You work too hard. And there's your constant dance of attendance on Mother, for which I'm grateful.

You have to forget all that. You have to relax.

CELIA I'm not very good at relaxing.

NELL While you're with us, you are *going* to relax. If not here, then where?

CELIA Yes. This would be the place for it.

NELL And that's all that's got you in this mood, this . . . nothing, this coincidence?

CELIA . . . Yes.

NELL Well, it's nothing.

Old people are like little children—they stir together everything they hear and present it as the *truth*.

My guess is, one night after work, you and your little
bag of take-out Chinese will stop at the local video store,
rent an obscure film from the thirties, and there you'll find
this entire plot. Jimmy Forever will be played by Dick
Powell.

You'll see.

CELIA Maybe.

NELL *(conclusive)* If there were such a thing as a Miri, why
did we never see her in the family pictures?

CELIA What family pictures?

(Beat. NELL deflates a bit.)

NELL Oh, the hell with all this, I've got a wedding to run, let's
have another drink!

CELIA Time for me to get home, I'm afraid.

NELL Stay. Stay here.

CELIA I *miss* the hotel, dear. I actively long for it.

NELL Promise me you'll try to have a good time while you're
here. Just . . . forget yourself for a few days, please?

CELIA I will *try*.

EV *bounds up to her.*

EV Can I drive you?

CELIA I've rented a car.

EV May I drive you home in it?

CELIA And how would you get home?

EV I could take a cab.

The time change, you must be tired.

CELIA I'm quite all right.

EV Oh. Okay.

Have a great time.

CELIA I'll only be going to sleep.
(Beat.)
EV Sleep wonderfully.

Lights.

Telephone rings.
CELIA *in the hotel room*/LAUREL *in her bedroom.*

CELIA Yes?
LAUREL Aunt Celia?
CELIA Laurel?
LAUREL It's not too late, is it?
CELIA No.
LAUREL I'm glad.
CELIA The bed's very luxe. You sort of want to stay awake admiring it.
LAUREL I've wanted to talk to you *all day*!
CELIA They give you these hand and body lotions; *very* compelling.
LAUREL God, I'm in agony!
CELIA And the ice bucket!
LAUREL Are you doing great?
CELIA *(disapproving noise)*
LAUREL I'm glad.
CELIA Did you say you were *in agony*?
LAUREL Yes.
CELIA Why?
LAUREL Oh God, oh God!

CELIA You're going to have to give me a little more than that, Laurel.

LAUREL I don't want to marry Ev.

CELIA What?

LAUREL It's like I'm—my whole life—I want to live my life! Do you know how young I am? *Fuck!*

CELIA Then why did you ever—

LAUREL I don't know, I don't know— I liked sleeping with him! I'm practically a virgin, Aunt Celia, if I've had sex with thirty other people, it's a lot. I want to do things, I want to move, I want to move out of here, it's so, the people are so—

CELIA I don't understand. You're marrying him because he's— the best of the thirty?— Or— I don't—

LAUREL No—no—that's glib. He—

He *has* something—but it's *bad*—

CELIA Is he evil in some—

LAUREL *Ev?* Oh God, oh *God*, no! He's—

If he were, maybe it would *work*!

I mean, he's not a bad *person*, he's like a bad effect that, if I marry him, will be like this life*long* bad effect, and— Oh, this is such a *mess*, Aunt Celia, I'm in such a *mess*!

CELIA Darling?

LAUREL Yes?

CELIA We're not especially close, why are we having this conversation?

LAUREL Who else—*who else*?

CELIA Your mother.

LAUREL My mother gives tours of malls— She— God— *God!*

CELIA The wedding is tomorrow.

LAUREL I'm not going to be here. I'm going to go someplace— I'm going to go some . . . *place*! New York!— Or—Israel!

CELIA But this *Ev*—

LAUREL My mother's sleeping with his father.

CELIA You know that.

LAUREL She tried to keep it a secret.

CELIA And you resent that.

LAUREL No, it's considerate—it's all so fucked up!

CELIA This is just: the night before the wedding.

LAUREL No it isn't—

CELIA Of course it is.

LAUREL Please, Aunt Celia, don't reduce me to who you think I
am.

CELIA I—wouldn't—

LAUREL My whole life has been like this great *thing*, like this
great *object* that everybody *poli*shes, and it can't just keep
*go*ing like that, can it, because then nothing will have ever
*hap*pened, which would be terrible, and if I marry Ev, it will
just be more of the same forever, which is a good thing, but
I know there's something else.

CELIA Darling—there isn't.

LAUREL You don't mean that. That's just . . . the next thing to
say.

    . . . Can I call you tomorrow?

CELIA . . . When you wake up?

LAUREL From New York. Please don't tell anyone!

CELIA Laurel—we both know you're not going to be in New
York tomorrow.

LAUREL You're right.

CELIA There.

LAUREL I'll call you from Israel.

CELIA Try Tel Aviv.

    There's shopping.

Lights.

NELL's *place*: CELIA *and* NELL; BEE *and* EV *are in formal wear.*

NELL And this is how you demonstrate your loathing!

CELIA Please, if you would listen to me—

NELL It was there, Celia, as plain as the nose on your face,
     right there on the screen: "Celia suggested Tel Aviv."

CELIA That was lighthearted—a mere quip, I—

NELL Well, who's laughing now?

CELIA Don't treat me like a daughter. "Who's laughing"—is that
     from your drug speech—?

NELL I have had it with you—

CELIA It was your daughter's idea— I thought she was—she
     had the jitters or—like something from a *movie*, for
     Christ's— How can you even tell the difference out here?

NELL She is *en route* to New York—and we have *tens* of
     thousands of dollars' worth of catered food, going to rot—

CELIA If you donate it to the homeless, I'm sure it's a write-off—

NELL What did she say to you? *What* did she *say* to you?

CELIA Gibberish.

BEE These things happen.

NELL Gibberish!

CELIA I didn't take it seriously. I told her Tel Aviv had good
     shopping.

NELL Shopping! Oh my God, she's on my credit card!

BEE The money's not the thing.

NELL Look at you: gloating.

CELIA No—

NELL How light-minded they are here, you're thinking. How
   tentative their commitments! How different we are back
   home. New York! Oh Christ, that child in New York!

CELIA She's twenty-one—

NELL Sans Baedeker and bodyguard—she'll be marauded!

CELIA It's the safest city in the country.

NELL She'll fall prey to white slavers!

CELIA The people at Disney are building "Crimewalk" so you
   can have an authentic urban experience—

NELL That poor innocent girl—

CELIA Innocent! Oh, enough, will you? She's slept with thirty men.

EV She has?

NELL So what? So what? How like you, Celia, to confuse sex
   with experience!

CELIA If everything I do is "so like me," does it really need to be
   remarked? Can't we just say I'm consistent and leave it at that?

BEE People have sex; even young women.

NELL If anything happens to her in that hellhole, I'll hold you
   responsible.

CELIA You know, you come from *Long* Island. It's not as if
   you're a native Californian.

NELL No one is a native Californian.

BEE I was born and raised in Santa Ana.

NELL *(angered by his non sequitur evenness)* Oh, and how
   was that for you, Bee?

BEE Nice, I enjoyed it.

CELIA Bee, do you ever say anything interesting?

BEE Nope. Don't have to. Got money.

NELL Oh, God help me, *guests* are arriving—*guests!*

CELIA Greet them.

NELL Well, I'm just going to *have* to, amn't I?

Bee!

BEE Yes?

NELL Come with me! We have to put a face on things.

BEE Yes.

NELL *(to* CELIA*)* You, later.

BEE *and* NELL *exit.*

CELIA *is alone with* EV.

Silence.

CELIA I'm sorry, Ev, quite sorry for any . . . discomfiture or . . .
 pain, even, this might be causing you.

EV *(sweetly)* Oh. Thanks.
 (Very long pause.)
 Is *R*omania the same thing as *R*umania?

(Pause.)

CELIA Yes.

EV Oh.
 (Beat; sadly.)
 Wow.

Lights.

Late; telephone rings.

CELIA Hello?

EV Is this too late?

CELIA No—

EV *(overlaps)* Sorry— I'm sor—

CELIA Who is this?

EV . . . It's—

CELIA Oh, Ev, it's—

EV —Ev—

CELIA It's you.

　　　How bizarre.

EV Could we talk a little?

CELIA Um, yes, sure.

(Pause.)

EV Could you start?

CELIA . . . Are you all right?

EV Uuummm . . .

　　　I'm sorry, I'm sorry I called, g'night.

CELIA *Ev—?*

He's hung up fast.
Later.
Phone rings.

CELIA Yes?

EV You don't sleep, right?

CELIA Ev.

EV You've got that thing where you don't sleep, right, what's it
　　called? Narcolepsy!

CELIA Insomnia—

EV *(overlaps)* Insomnia, that's what I meant!

CELIA How did you know?

EV Oh, you're all talking fast? And your eyes?

CELIA Do my eyes have rings beneath them?

EV Yeah.

(Pause.)

CELIA Deep black ones?

EV Yeah.

(Pause.)

CELIA This has been a stressful time.

    I mean, they're not permanent.

    They're reversible.

EV Oh, sure.

    (Beat.)

    I know this guy you can use.

CELIA This—?

EV My mom goes to him—

CELIA Guy—?

EV Laurel's mom, too. That's how we met.

CELIA A surgeon, do you mean a surgeon?

EV We were like in the waiting room, and they were all, these bandages? And so we each started pulling on the wrong mom, because the handbags? They were the same, too? So that's how we . . .

    We were so *laugh*ing when that . . . *(He trails off sadly.)*

CELIA Ev?

EV I'm sorry I called.

(He hangs up fast.)

Lights.

Telephone rings.

EV You still have insomnia, right?

CELIA Ev.

EV I'm not waking you, right?

CELIA Please don't hang up this time.

EV Do you want to go someplace?

(Beat.)

CELIA Meaning now?

EV We could drive.

CELIA It's some o'clock of the morning—

EV I know this all-night place?

CELIA Where would we drive?

EV We could get a Jamba Juice.

CELIA I don't understand.

EV Or a coffee.

CELIA I'm perplexed.

EV You could explain things to me.

CELIA I don't understand.

EV You could tell me things.

CELIA What things?

EV You could tell me why she walked out on me.

(Beat.)

CELIA I don't know why, Ev.

EV You could tell me why she left me.

CELIA I don't know why, Ev—

EV You could tell me why . . .

CELIA . . .

   . . .

   Ev?

EV I love her so much!

   Shit!

   I'm sorry!

He hangs up quickly.
Telephone rings.

EV Or we could drive to the ocean.

CELIA The ocean?

EV Open all night, ha-ha.

CELIA Why me?

EV We could drive to Laguna.

CELIA Why are you calling me? There must be other people
who—

EV Or Dana Point—

CELIA Your friends or—your father or—

EV You know things.

CELIA I'm sorry, Ev, I don't. I told you I don't know why
she—

EV But you know *things*!

> (*Beat.*)

> After you left? My dad? He was all "There, there." And
Laurel's mom was all "Fifty pounds of spiced ham!" And my
friends? Got pizza? And I . . . like . . . ?

> You know things.

(Pause.)

CELIA Is it very cold out?

EV Maybe.

CELIA I thought you were all terribly sensitive to that. I
thought your blood thinned.

EV Not mine. Mine is warm.

(Pause.)

CELIA Can you give me twenty minutes?

EV Sure.

CELIA Fifteen.

Lights.

In the car.

CELIA What a snappy little roadster!

EV Driving's good.

CELIA Windy.

      I don't suppose you ever read Nancy Drew.

EV I don't know who that is.

CELIA She had a snappy little roadster. Do you know the Hardy Boys?

EV No.

CELIA She was their little sister. Unofficially.

      My girlhood, forgive me.

EV Okay.

      (They drive.)

      What was the Anschluss?

CELIA . . . Hitler annexed Austria.

EV During the war?

CELIA Yes.

      This looks like New England to me.

EV It's new.

CELIA This looks like something phony in New England.

EV It's kinda nice. You make a right, and there's the ocean.

CELIA One block over?

EV There's benches.

      I ate there once.

CELIA *(not having heard)* What?

EV Pancakes.

CELIA Um, all right.

Ev, where are we going?

EV Dunno, but do you mind if I go really, really fast?

CELIA Please.

> *(He floors it.)*
>
> Wheeeee!

Lights.

On a bench.

CELIA Look at this.

EV Uh-huh.

CELIA The sky.

EV You keep seeing it.

CELIA Yes.

EV Everywhere.

CELIA It must get quite annoying after a while.

EV . . . This one time, Laurel and I . . . ?

(Pause.)

CELIA Do you surf?

EV No.

CELIA Oh!

EV I Jet Ski.

CELIA Don't people die from that rather a lot?

EV Other people.

CELIA Not you.

EV I wouldn't know how.

> *(Beat.)*
>
> I trained. I took this lesson.

(Beat.)

This one time, we went north? Laurel and I?

We took a tour of the north?

CELIA Alaska?

EV San Francisco? South of San Francisco? This hike this time?

CELIA Yes.

EV And there were these lights?

They were . . .

(Beat.)

And one time I got poison oak, and Colby and Caitlin, they were all *"We're* not getting in the Jacuzzi with you," but Laurel was like: "The *chlor*ine," and she didn't even mind my body.

CELIA Your—

EV It was all over . . . *stuff*, red, from the stuff and stuff.

But she'd look at it.

That was . . .

(Beat.)

And sometimes we'd come to the beach, and we wouldn't even *do* anything . . .

(Beat.)

CELIA Because of the poison oak?

EV No. This was another time. *That* time, too.

(Beat.)

We'd go to the beach, and the ocean just makes me want to keep talking, so I just shut up?

And she's all "What are you thinking," and this that and the other, and I'm like "What?"

And so she gets this look.

Like "Whoa, you're an idiot."

And so I keep shutting up because, like, I figure, my *odds*?

And then the ocean?
(wanting to say everything)
It . . .
(Silence. The silence gets deeper and deeper; dark, inward.)
CELIA . . . Ev?
EV I'm ashamed of myself.

Lights.

An all-night deli.

CELIA This place. I wouldn't have imagined . . .
EV Nobody much knows about it. I'm like, sometimes I get
   hungry? Cause I don't sleep much? And I get in my car.
   They've got Jewish food.
CELIA Delicatessen.
EV Oh. Did I— I wasn't being prejudice or anything . . .
CELIA I know that.
EV I like chopped chicken livers!
CELIA Good.
EV Laurel sometimes . . .
CELIA . . . Why don't you sleep?
EV Dunno.
   (He starts tapping his foot.)
   Do you like this music?
CELIA . . . Yes.
EV Sinatra.
   I think he's gonna have a career surge now that he's dead.
   Like Tony Bennett.

(Beat.)
I dunno why I don't sleep.
. . . The coffee?

CELIA Ah.

EV I don't think it's that.

CELIA One summer—these were my teens—I would go to the
local diner with chums and drink ten cups of coffee at one
in the morning and never fall asleep and I didn't know why. I
thought I was in love.

EV With who?

CELIA . . . It was the coffee.

EV So you were really beautiful then, right?
(Pause.)

CELIA *(flustered)* Um, no, no—

EV Oh. *(with a smile as if they both know she's lying)*
Okay.

CELIA . . . There might have been a moment.
But I did nothing with it.
. . .
Ev?
It's some o'clock of the morning.

EV Uh-huh.

CELIA You are the chauffeur this evening.

EV We can go if you want to.

CELIA Thank you.

EV Please don't want to.

CELIA I mean, this is starting to be improper.

EV *(laughs sweetly)* Are you like that?

CELIA Like—?

EV Improper. I mean: "This is improper."

CELIA . . . I have forgotten how I am. I have misplaced myself.

Clearly, I am not in this dive on this beach at this hour with you; *that* is an absurd suggestion.

EV You hate it around here, right?

CELIA I—

It's lovely.

EV Don't say that.

CELIA Do *you* hate it here?

EV I could learn!

. . .

Tell me things.

CELIA *What* things? What things do you want me to tell you?

EV Anything!

. . . Do you work?

CELIA . . . Yes.

EV That must be good. Is that good?

CELIA Yes. Very good.

Thank God for it—it's what I do.

Do *you* work?

EV I'm supposed to finish school, then, like, I'm going in with my dad?

CELIA And what is it he does now?

EV Nothing.

Waitress!

An elderly woman comes over. CELIA *scans the menu.*

Could I get the chopped chicken livers? But not the sandwich? The appetizer portion? But instead of rye bread? Could I get bagel chips?

(The waitress nods.)

(to CELIA*)* Do you want something?

CELIA *looks up, sees the waitress, and is spellbound at the sight of her. Pause.*

CELIA Coffee.

EV Um, oh, and instead of bagel chips? Which I wanted instead of rye bread, remember? Could I have squaw bread?

The waitress leaves.

CELIA My grandmother used to wash money.
EV So did my grandfather!
    In Swiss banks.
CELIA This was in a soapy solution.
EV Oh! That's—another thing—
CELIA On the Lower East Side of Manhattan.
    Not yet the East Village.
    Still, I expect, pushcarts.
    She would run what she took to be literally filthy lucre
    through a tub of suds and then hang the bills with
    clothespins from a clothesline.
    Outside?
    On the tenement fire escape?
    Daring passersby to snatch them away from her?
    Did she stand guard? Did she have a weapon?
    Their faces were their weapons, those women.
    Those old immigrant women.
    Skin like corduroy.
    Blazing eyes.
. . .
    The coins she would lay on a cloth towel. To air-dry.
    (Beat.)

I have one memory of her.

When I was four? Five? Six?

And she had come to stay for a weekend.

She washed her face.

That's my memory.

We were already in Hewlett.

Her eyes were gray, a lovely shade of gray.

She had been a young widow. This didn't occur to me then.

She was old as no one ever gets anymore.

A little while later, she was off to a home.

Once I set foot in the lobby.

A menagerie of the impossibly old. Beyond everything but suffering.

But why was I there?

Why wasn't I in the car, with my father, as we usually did it? Had my mother spent too long with my grandmother, had my father gone to fetch her?

And where was my sister?

The ancient in their wheelchairs.

One woman—I think a woman—reached toward me—or at any rate out. She had no eyes, or useless or closed eyes, and her mouth . . .

And a moan came from her, only not from her throat—it seemed to be a separate sound, and she was lost inside it. And a stench, which at that age doesn't come from the flesh but from the bones and, like the moaning, really from nowhere.

And I was . . . all of six.

All of five, or four.

And upstairs, my grandmother.

Was she dying then?

Was that why my mother spent too long? And had my father chased her, surly, impatient? Was this a cause of the trouble between them, one of the causes of the trouble that came later, or had already begun, and would one day be all there was?

And when they came down and rescued me . . .

I don't remember that part.

Years passed.

I remember my grandmother washing her face.

A bitter woman. Unloved by her daughters.

By two of her daughters.

One day she died. In that place. The call came.

(Beat.)

What brought me to that story?

(Beat.)

What always brings me to these stories?

EV I think it's terrible what the Swiss did.

(CELIA *looks up.*)

I think they should give the Jewish people back their stuff, and things, don't you?

(Beat.)

CELIA What are you ashamed of?

EV Huh?

CELIA What do you—of all people—have to be ashamed of?

EV *(trying to answer)* Oh.

I dunno.

You know.

Whatever.

Things . . . and stuff.

(Beat.)

CELIA May we go back now?

EV We—can't—we—*ordered*—we have to—

CELIA We can pay and—

EV Help me!

CELIA . . . what?

EV I dunno.

CELIA Ev—

EV Get to sleep. I can't sleep.

CELIA How? How do I help you sleep?

EV I dunno.

We could go to the beach? After we eat? We could go to
the beach and you could hold me?

CELIA *That* would be too bizarre—

EV *(panicked)* I can't sleep! I can't sleep, and usually that's okay
because I can think about Laurel, but now I can't, and I think I'm
gonna go crazy, so please please please don't leave me—don't—

CELIA *(overlaps slightly, covering his hands with hers)* All
right—yes—it's all right—I won't leave.

He grows quiet.
Pause.

EV This one time, Laurel and I . . . ?

Quietly, almost imperceptibly, he starts to cry.
CELIA *moves closer to him, awkwardly holds him.*
After a moment, tentatively, he kisses her.

CELIA *(pulling back a little)* Of course not.
(EV moves away a little, too, and looks down.)

EV Oh, okay.

The waitress arrives with their order. CELIA *stares at her.*

WAITRESS *Wuss?*

Lights.

LAUREL, *solo.*

LAUREL Dear Mom:

    I'm sending this from this place where you can sort of get coffee but there are also these terminals.

    I never got to Israel. I was such a mess when I left that I forgot my passport, so I've stayed the whole time in New York.

    Don't worry—nothing's happened.

    I've been staying in the cheapest hotel I could find that wouldn't drive you crazy; I've been looking around.

    I'm a tourist.

    Something did happen, but it wasn't in the city.

    Don't worry! It wasn't a crime! I haven't been the victim of a crime, there isn't any crime— I can't find a crime *anywhere.*

    I'm safe.

    The thing that happened, it . . .

    (Beat. She shakes her head, deleting this.)

    I hope you're well.

    I'm coming home.

    I wish I'd gone to Israel.

    I miss everything.

Lights.

CELIA, NELL, *and* BEE.

NELL I have just heard, and I am just appalled!

CELIA By what? By what this time?

NELL Did you spend the night with Ev? With Bee's son?
    With my daughter's fiancé? With your niece's fiancé, Ev?

CELIA Don't stop there. I think there are some club
  memberships you may have left out.

BEE Nell—

NELL Shut up, Bee, this doesn't concern you.

BEE I think it does.

CELIA You were the father when the cast list was read, weren't
  you?

BEE I think so. I'm not sure; it was dizzying.

NELL Was it *carnal?*

CELIA . . . !
    Who *are* you?
    "Carnal"?

NELL Well?

CELIA Nell.

NELL *Well, was it?*

CELIA . . . Of course not.
    It never is with me.

BEE Surely sometimes.

NELL *Did you spend the night with him?*

CELIA We took a ride in his car.
    He wanted to talk.

We stopped certain places.

The beach at last.

He slept. I did not.

The night passed, the sun rose.

We saw it in each other's company.

Yes, I suppose: we spent the night.

NELL *makes a confounded sound.* CELIA *laughs.*

NELL Do not laugh at me!

CELIA I wouldn't.

NELL You do. You do. You eternally do.

You came here—so flustered, so bemused. I was certain you were having a breakdown of some kind. You know, that runs in the family, Bee—*not me.*

(to CELIA*)* You laugh at the tours I give, you laugh at the parties I plan, you laugh at the cocktails I serve precisely on the hour.

Well, these are my ceremonies, Celia, they're how I mark my time, and if all you have for them is . . . contempt—

CELIA I don't have contempt for them, Nell. I envy and admire you. You've found your niche—you're the historian of a place that's fourteen months old—what a coup!

NELL I *have to do something*! Do you know what it's *like* here? *The afternoons are eighteen hours long!*

CELIA Nell—

NELL Young men *will* screw older women, they just like to, it's their favorite thing, don't listen, Bee. It's not preposterous of me to infer that—

CELIA But it is—

NELL I will not be defied!

Oh look—oh look—I am going in and having a bath and a cocktail. I trust neither of you will interrupt my solitude unless a whistle has been sounded or a flag waved.

She exits.
Once she's gone:

BEE She's good at exiting.

(CELIA *smiles and shakes her head.*)

You're fine?

CELIA I am.

BEE So what did you do, really?

CELIA Conversed.

BEE Conversed? *Ev*, too?

CELIA Yes. A good deal, in fact.

Such a sweet boy.

He talks and talks and talks and there's never any more of him.

BEE Contrary to what you probably think, I have worked very hard in my time.

CELIA I'm sure of it—

BEE As did my father before me.

Worked *very* hard.

So that one day we might produce a sweet child with an uncomplicated life.

Poor Ev.

(He crosses to the liquor tray and moves to mix drinks.)

CELIA Did your father ever work with someone named Jimmy Forever?

BEE Jimmy Forever?

CELIA Yes.

BEE That can't be.

CELIA I didn't think so—

BEE That's like one of those Warner Brothers gangster
names—

CELIA Nell said that, too.

BEE Well, I mean.

(He reaches for a decanter, then stops.)

Constant.

CELIA Pardon?

BEE James Constant was his name. Not "Forever," merely . . .
"Constant." He was my father's first partner.

Right at the beginning.

Is that who you mean?

CELIA Yes, I think so.

BEE Did you know him?

CELIA He was engaged to my mother's sister.

BEE Really? Jimmy Constant was engaged to your aunt? That's—

CELIA Not exactly, no. I mean, she didn't get to be my aunt.
She died a few months before I was born.

BEE Oh, I'm . . .

But that's something, isn't it? That's really something.

CELIA Yes, it is . . . *some*thing, isn't it?

BEE . . . Yes.

CELIA . . . Did you ever meet him?

BEE I think I did. He retired early, but I think when I was a
child, I— Yes, I'm sure of it.

CELIA What was he like?

BEE He seemed . . . perfectly nice.

(Beat.)

He was . . .

He thinks a moment, realizes he has no more information,
shrugs, and smiles, returning to mixing drinks.

CELIA Are you truly Everett Beekin the Seventh?

BEE I am.

CELIA And Ev is the Eighth?

BEE He is.

CELIA It's nice keeping track of one's ancestors and all, but
eight generations, I'm sorry, is a mania.

BEE It's only four.

CELIA Am I innumerate?

BEE There's a story behind that. *(thoughtful, realizing)* It
might interest you.

CELIA Doubtful.

BEE But possible. May I tell it?

    *(*CELIA *shrugs.)*

    Once upon a time—

CELIA Oh, *truly*?

BEE *(undeflected; fixing and handing her a drink during*
this) —there were two sisters who lived in St. Louis, circa
nineteen aught four. In a lovely old wooden house in the
middle of a lazy tree-shaded street with, of course, a porch
and a swing in the yard, and all the standard accoutrements.
They hadn't married but by all accounts were too vivacious
and good-looking to be called spinsters. Even under the
gaze of the day, which was . . . cruel and . . . assessing, they
were . . . something more.

    Witches, some said.

    Well.

    There was a room in their house, on the parlor floor that
had for many years remained empty. It was a white room

with a painted white wooden floor and an iron bed and nothing else. And after many years, the sisters decided to let it. Rooms were at a premium then—

CELIA Because of the fair—

BEE —because—exactly!—because of the fair. And a young man came, whose name was Justin Something—

CELIA —to be a worker at the fair—

BEE *(overlaps)* —to be a worker at the fair, yes; and took the room.

CELIA And he was handsome.

BEE No pictures exist.

CELIA Pity.

BEE But we *presume* he was handsome.

CELIA They always are in stories like this.

BEE And things were fine at first.

The sisters cooked for him, and did his laundry, and at night they would sit, the three of them, and drink coffee, and smoke.

And they would tell him tales of their brother.

CELIA Whose room this once had been.

BEE Whose room this once had been.

Everett—

CELIA Ah!

BEE —had gone with a delegation to China! Everett was the writer of famous novels! Everett was a doctor—a traveler—a Don Juan—a minister!—detailed and contradictory scenarios—breathtaking in their precision and unlikeliness.

And at first Justin Something was quite taken in—

CELIA But then—

BEE But then it occurred to him that Everett was having too many lives. And one night—gently—*joshingly*—he challenged the sisters on this point. Everett was the younger sibling, the ladies themselves were none too old, and even if he were a *mad*man, he simply would not have had *time* to explore so many radically differing pursuits.

CELIA Whereupon—

BEE Whereupon it was revealed that there were, in fact, *five* Everett Beekins.

CELIA Five of them!

BEE Yes, five. Five brothers named Everett.

CELIA How's *that* for a lack of imagination?

BEE "But then why," Justin Something wondered, "do you never receive a letter from them? Or a visit? Why don't they send fruit?"

CELIA Whereupon it transpired . . .

BEE When we think of the turn of this century—

CELIA Something I never do—

BEE —doesn't it seem there was a small quiet patch?

A couple of peaceful and leisurely years?

When we took to our porches and basked in the moment?

CELIA I'm sure there's a war you're leaving out.

BEE Large houses—even not-so-large houses—had a room, often, a room in the front and on the ground floor for quick access, in which family members languished. From the bugs, the viruses, the incurable contagions that were rampant at the time and decimated many—most?—families.

But these two sisters were strong.

And so they watched as their five little brothers succumbed in succession. Each having been born to replace the last. One living a day. One three years.

And as each died—always, cruelly, in spring or summer,
when flags were flown from gabled windows and the
neighbors promenaded in their whites—the sisters would
turn to each other and say: "He would have been a
statesman. A doctor. A visionary. A roué."

And they lived on. Witches.

CELIA And Justin Something—

BEE My grandfather.

My father was a bastard.

I know everybody says that, but in my case, it's the case.

CELIA Did they make love the night he was told the story? He
and the—younger?—

BEE Older—

CELIA (surprised) Older? . . . sister?

BEE Yes.

Or at least I tell it that way.

CELIA In the room where all the babies had died.

BEE On that lousy iron bed, are you nuts? The mattress had
no give. They went up to her room. Proper goose-down
pillows; they had a good time.

(Beat.)

My father told me that story only just before he died.

(Beat.)

His mother told it to him just before *she* died.

(Beat.)

I still haven't told Ev.

CELIA And when you do . . .

BEE I'll know I'm going to die.

Lights.

At first we just see NELL.

NELL Oh yay! Oh lovely! Oh Laurel! But why didn't you call?
Why didn't you call us? I could have picked you up—

And LAUREL *appears.*

LAUREL I didn't want you to bother any more than—
NELL It wouldn't have been a bother—but you're back! You're
safe! Thank God!
LAUREL I'm so sorry, I'm so sorry I ran out—
NELL No—no recriminations.
LAUREL Thank you.
NELL No guilting my girl.
LAUREL Thank you.
NELL We'll say nothing of the guests—
LAUREL Thank you—
NELL We'll say nothing of the credit-card abuse, we'll say
nothing of the catering costs, we'll say nothing of the
ham.

BEE *and* CELIA *enter.* LAUREL *looks at them.*

LAUREL I'm . . . very tired—
NELL Are you hungry? Can Glinda get you something?
LAUREL No, I don't want anything to eat—
BEE Ev's here, Laurel. Can I get him?
LAUREL Give me a little while, please.
BEE Do you *want* to see Ev?
LAUREL *(emotionally)* Oh, I do, I do.
NELL Imagine if she'd said those words two days ago! But no!

My baby is not to know guilt. Where did you go, Laurel? What did you see?

LAUREL I went to the island.

NELL To the island?

LAUREL To Hewlett.

I went to Grandma's. Grandma Anna's.

NELL She didn't call—she didn't tell us. Is she very far gone, Laurel? Is that it? Did she seem very far gone to—

LAUREL I went to Grandma Anna's, Celia.

CELIA I see.

LAUREL I went to Grandma Anna's.

NELL Yes, darling, you've told us.

LAUREL I went to Grandma Anna's, and she—

EV *enters. He and* LAUREL *just freeze a moment, looking at each other. Then she crosses to him, and he holds her tightly.*

EV Oh—thank you.

LAUREL *(to* NELL*)* I'm going to my room and talk with Ev for a minute, but then come see me, all right? In a minute?

NELL We can talk later—

LAUREL *(leaving with* EV*)* No. Just a minute. Half a minute—

NELL All right—do you want something to eat?

LAUREL No.

She and EV *are gone.*

NELL *(calling)* There's ham!

LAUREL *(offstage)* No, thank you!

NELL Well, she's jet-lagged and a little weird, but she's back, she's safe, thank God!

CELIA I think I'd like a drink.

NELL I think we could all use a little drink right about now—I'll make them—

CELIA No. Go to Laurel. She wants to talk to you—

NELL I'll let them be alone awhile.

CELIA No. She wants to talk to you now—

NELL She won't once they're alone.

CELIA Yes. She will.

NELL Oh, really, you *know* this?

CELIA Yes.

NELL Given the havoc you've wreaked this weekend, I hardly think you're in a position—

CELIA Nell, it's important.

NELL Celia—

CELIA I'm right—

NELL I—

CELIA This once, will you do what I ask of you? *(quietly)* Please?

NELL *looks at her, then exits.*

BEE All this mystery—all this *dra*ma!

CELIA Do you know, is there a flight later to New York?

BEE You're not leaving.

CELIA Yes. I am.

BEE But this wedding may come off after all—

CELIA I won't be wanted there.

BEE Of course you will.

Of *course* you will.

CELIA No, my holiday is over, I'm afraid.
    (laughs, surprised)
    Oh, isn't that funny?
    Isn't that something?
    This has been a holiday!
(She laughs again.)

Lights.

CELIA *alone.*
NELL *enters. A moment.*

CELIA Oh—attack me now, break the suspense.
NELL I'm not going to attack you, dear.
    It's all right, dear.
(Beat.)
CELIA I had come to surprise her.
    I came every Wednesday night on the five-eleven train,
  like clockwork. It always surprised her.
    I rang the bell, so as to surprise but not to startle.
    No answer.
    I used my key.
    She wasn't anywhere.
    I waited.
    Hours, as it turned out.
    Well, you know, there wasn't anyone to call. She hadn't
  made friends with the new neighbors. *All* the neighbors *are*
  new.
    Eventually, I heard a scratching noise in the basement.

I thought a stray dog was clawing at the window, that small window.

I went around to the side of the house, there was nothing.

So I checked the basement.

She looked like something that had been collapsed and heaped somewhere out of the way—a tent or a canvas bag—truly, that's what I thought I saw.

She'd fallen and passed out. She'd been bleeding internally for hours, several hours, but right before dying, she stirred and scratched violently at the floor in an effort to get to the stairs.

. . .

. . .

There's nothing *in* that basement, you know; there's absolutely no reason to go there.

. . .

. . .

I knew I had to get her buried within twenty-four hours.

I knew that *had* to happen.

We still do that, don't we?

. . .

. . .

I calculated you couldn't make it in time. That this would put the kibosh on a very extravagant wedding party. I calculated I didn't need to tell you until it had all come off splendidly.

And then, of course, the other thing happened, and I guess I missed the moment.

. . .

And it was mine!

It was mine!

You can have everything else, but this much belongs to me!

NELL Did you bury her within twenty-four hours?

CELIA Of course I did.

Time to spare. Then next day to you.

NELL Well, then.

That's all right, then.

CELIA . . . Is it?

NELL Even appropriate.

Thank you. I'm grateful to you.

. . .

She had a good long life.

CELIA She had a *long* life.

NELL And good.

CELIA She had *nothing*! That marriage—was a disaster—she had the house—the house was monstrous—she grew old in it—half the time she didn't remember her *name*—

NELL *(simply)* None of this is true.

(This stops CELIA.*)*

But no—you must know—you did exactly the right thing.

(Beat.)

CELIA Ah.

(Beat.)

A sound of laughter. EV *and* LAUREL *enter. They are touching, leaning in to each other; really the only word for it is "playing."*

CELIA Ev and Laurel look as if nothing's happened—as if nothing's happened between them—

NELL Well, nothing has, really—
CELIA But—
NELL Nothing has.

     They'll just pick up where they left off.

     Costing me a fortune, but . . . *c'est la—*
CELIA Nell—!
NELL It's all right, dear.

     It's all fine.
CELIA *(almost a plea)* . . . Nell?
NELL It's all right, dear.

     It's all fine.
(Beat.)
CELIA Oh.

By now BEE *has entered. He stands upstage with a drink,*
looking out at the water, satisfied.
CELIA *slowly turns a full circle, taking in* BEE, *then* EV *and*
LAUREL, *then her sister, and finally the water. All is calm.*
There's nothing for her anywhere.
A moment. She collects herself, then:

     I am *such* an ass!

     What am I looking at again?

     Is this an inlet, or a cove, or some certain beach with a
     name?
NELL No, dear, it's the Pacific.

     You're looking at the Pacific.

And they look at it.

                    FADE.